Healing

Healing

A Spiritual Adventure

by Mary E. Peterman

FORTRESS PRESS   Philadelphia

The quotation at the beginning of Chapter 1 is from the Today's English Version of the Psalms. Copyright © American Bible Society 1972. The quotations at the beginning of Chapters 3, 4, 5, 6, 7, 8 and 10 are from the Today's English Version of the New Testament. Copyright © American Bible Society 1966, 1971. Used by permission.

Library of Congress Catalog Card Number 74-80416

ISBN 0-8006-1086-5

Second printing 1976

6229J76   Printed in U.S.A.   1-1086

To Dick—

Without whom I would be incomplete

Contents

Preface

"My husband has a circulatory condition. He has had such pain for the past six weeks and has become so discouraged he actually cries.

"The doctor says an operation may be necessary on the aorta, or his leg might have to be amputated. Jim has lost twenty pounds and has reached the point where he cannot walk at all."

The letter was from a woman requesting prayer for her husband. Sometime later she wrote: "Mrs. Peterman, prayers have been answered. The day Jim was supposed to see the surgeon he suddenly was able to walk again. He has been improving ever since. It has been a very moving experience for all of us."

That's healing of the body.

A seventy year old woman was at the point of suicide. Her deep depression had her in tears most of the day. In her golden years she felt rejected by her only daughter. Her niece suggested, "Aunt Jennie, come stay with me and my family for a month or so; let's see if we can help."

After the aunt's arrival, the niece and her family prayed for her and with her. They opened up a line of communication between Aunt Jennie and her daughter. Mother and daughter discovered that each was feeling rejected by the other. They are now living together—happily. The mother says, "The turning point came at the second healing service I attended. As the pastor laid his hands on my head and prayed, I felt a great peace. From that time on everything was all right."

That's healing of the mind.

"To think that I spent my entire ministry believing my peer group. They told me the gifts of the Spirit were only for New Testament times."

Tears filled the eyes of the eighty-two year old retired pastor as he voiced his lament.

Forty-five minutes of conversation with him revealed that he was frantically seeking for some gift of the Spirit. He was emotionally torn apart by his quest.

As we were about to part he said, "Mary, I wish you could meet my Amy. She is confined at home now. We have been married for almost fifty years, and we're so in love. It gets better all the time."

Now I had tears in *my* eyes. "But then you have the greatest gift of all; you have love."

"Why, I never thought of that," he mused. "I feel better already."

That's healing of the spirit.

As I have traveled across the land speaking about the healing Christ, as I have read and answered hundreds of letters and listened to people pour out their hearts, as I have seen churches filled with worshippers at healing missions—I have become convinced of the validity of healing services as a regular aspect of the church's total ministry.

This book is intended as a modest witness to the healing love of the Great Physician in my life and to the power of his Holy Spirit working through the community of faith and prayer.

My hope is that you, the reader, will consider what follows with an open mind. If you believe that Christ is raised from the dead, that he forgives and loves and blesses, can you not also believe that he heals in body, mind, and spirit?

1. Back from the Depths

> I cried to you for help, Lord my God,
>   and you healed me.
> You brought me back from the world of
>   the dead.
> I was with those who go down to the
>   depths below,
>   but you restored my life.
> Sing praise to the Lord,
>   his faithful people!
> Remember what the Holy One has done
>   and give him thanks!
>
> Ps. 30:2-4

Coming "back from the depths," as the Psalmist well knew, is quite an adventure. Let me tell you about it as I "remember" it.

"Pastor, Laura is going to the Mayo Clinic on Monday. She has all the symptoms of multiple sclerosis. Do you think we could pray for her at the service this Sunday morning? I mean have her come to the altar rail and kneel and be prayed for personally rather than be named in the general prayer of the church?"

Jane was intent as she looked at my husband, the pastor of St. John's Church in Summit, New Jersey. Jane was Laura's shepherd, the person assigned to guide her through her first year as a member of our parish.

"I'd be happy to do that," my husband responded. Laura's pastor knew that she was twenty-seven years old and the mother of two small children, but he hadn't known about the physical problem.

Further conversation revealed that Laura herself had requested this prayer opportunity; yet she was reluctant to go alone to the altar rail and kneel before the congregation. So, it was decided that a general invitation would be issued in the service to anyone

1

who had a personal need and desired personal prayer. Emphasis would be placed on the concern of the whole congregation, the body of Christ, for each of its members.

This had never been done before in our Lutheran parish. It represented such a dramatic change from our formal, liturgical worship that I was positive no one else would respond to the invitation to "come forward."

The congregation that Sunday morning was quite unaware of what was coming. At the point in the service where we have the general prayer, the pastor briefly explained what was to take place and extended the invitation to anyone who would like personal prayer. Twenty-six people came forward!

I was amazed. And so were many others. Among the twenty-six were staid "pillars of the church," people whom I never dreamed would get up and go forward.

As a result of that Sunday morning, my husband was given an opportunity to minister to his parishioners more fully. One couple came to him with a marital problem, a young lady brought an emotional problem, and numerous people spoke of physical problems. In several instances counseling resulted, counseling that might otherwise not have occurred.

As for Laura, she went to the Mayo Clinic where examination revealed no evidence of multiple sclerosis. She was given a course of therapy and sent home.

Our parish had experienced the healing power of the living Christ in answer to prayer. We were grateful, of course, but most of us naturally assumed that there had been a wrong diagnosis in the first place. Every once in awhile someone would suggest that we make the prayer opportunity available again, but we just didn't get around to doing it.

About six months later, Jane came back to the pastor to tell him of her own experience with the healing Christ. She had been holding her small baby when the child thrust his little hand into her face and scratched the cornea of her eye with his tiny, sharp fingernail. She went to an eye specialist time and again, but the

2

scratch defied healing. Finally, Jane decided to travel to Philadelphia to a healing service at St. Stephen's Episcopal Church where Dr. Alfred W. Price had been conducting healing services every Thursday for thirty years. She knelt at the altar with an injured eye. She arose with a healed eye. The following day Jane went back to the specialist without telling him what had happened. He peered into the eye and said, "Oh, I'm looking in the wrong eye." "No," she said smiling, "that's the eye all right, but it has been healed." When she finished relating the story, her doctor said quite simply, "It's a miracle."

Thus I encountered Christ as healer a second time. At St. John's Church, however, we still did nothing about offering personal prayer opportunities and a healing ministry.

Some months later, in March of 1969, I entered the hospital myself for what was to be routine surgery. In the course of the operation, cancer was discovered. The doctor spoke with my husband afterwards: "It's grim. The probability of her recovery is not good." My husband responded, "In your profession you speak of probabilities; in mine, we speak of miracles."

The next day was Sunday. At all the three services the parish was told of my situation. Prayers were offered and the body of Christ responded to their sick member—me.

Two laymen of the parish, both with Ph.D.'s in chemistry, came to my husband later that day and told him they wanted to have a special prayer service for me on Wednesday evening. The two laymen prepared the service. Everyone in the parish was called and invited to attend. The place was packed—and Christ was present. Many people told me later that they were aware of his presence in a way they had never experienced before.

I knew that this service was to be held, though at the time I did not know that a malignancy had been discovered. In fact, I felt wonderful. As I lay in my hospital bed that Wednesday evening during the hour of the service, I kept thinking, "Something is happening to me." For the first time in my life I was aware of the power of the Holy Spirit within me, a resource I had never before called upon or used.

3

HEALING

On Thursday the pathologist's report came back. It was, as the surgeon knew, positive. My husband told me of the results and assured me of his confidence that I would recover. I was blessed in having the support of his optimistic and positive attitude. My children also supported me. Thus, the body of Christ closest to me, my family and my congregation, came to my aid.

I asked my doctor quite frankly, "What advice can you give me?" He turned from the bed, slumped in the chair, and said, "If I were you, I'd get my papers in order." His remark had an air of finality about it.

Thoughts tumble through one's mind at a time like that. "I will tell no one," I thought. "I don't want anyone feeling sorry for me." Yet somewhere within me the Holy Spirit was saying, "But you are part of the body of Christ. Let that body respond to your need." So I wrote a letter to the parish:

Dear Friends of Saint John's,

I am making a remarkably speedy recovery from the surgery I had last Saturday, and I am grateful to all of you for your cards, flowers, love—and especially your prayers.

I have decided to tell you that the doctor did find a malignancy. He is confident. I am confident. He has put me on a new drug that will discourage stray cells, should there be any, from implanting. Since this drug can affect the white blood cells, it will be necessary for me to stay in the hospital for another week as a blood count must be taken each day until he can determine a balanced dosage.

Since I do not feel sorry for myself, I do not expect you to feel sorry either. I am just thankful for the miracles of modern surgery, drugs, and care which are part of God's creation.

Most of all, I am thankful for the healing power of God and the miracles he can perform.

Thanks a million for all this wonderful sustaining prayer you have poured out on my behalf.

Now come on, all you people, SMILE.

Love,

Mary

4

How was I able to write such a letter? As I look at it now I marvel at the power that is present when we need it. A verse of scripture floated into my mind. It became my "anchor verse." I used it every time I needed it—hundreds of times: "I can do all things through Christ who strengthens me."

My daughter-in-law, Mary Ann, agreed to take a week of her vacation to stay with me once I arrived home: "I'll make a deal with you. I'll stay with you now, if you will come and stay with me when we have our first baby." She kept her part of the bargain; I kept mine. Two years later I *did* stay with her when Christopher was born. I learned from my daughter-in-law the importance of giving the sick person purpose and hope.

During my convalescence my husband insisted that I get out of the house, go with him on errands, take rides. One morning, as I was waiting for him in a Sears parking lot, I opened the glove compartment and a book fell out. The title didn't excite me—*A Reporter Finds God Through Spiritual Healing**—but, having nothing else to do, I started to skim through the book.

It is the autobiographical story of Emily Gardner Neal, a professional journalist who set out to write an article discrediting spiritual healing. In the course of her research she was converted and is now a leader in the field of healing.

Jane, the woman who had been involved in the two previous healing experiences at St. John's, had given this book to my husband. It "just happened" to come into my hands at the right time. The book opened my heart and mind to Christ as healer. Further, it made clear the important place of healing services in parish life.

Prior to my surgery, our choir director had asked me to speak on "Art in Worship" at our adult forum on a Sunday morning in May. But the forum date was only eight weeks after my surgery and, having been treated by chemotherapy, I was in a constant state of nausea.

*Bibliographical notes appear at the back of the book beginning on page 89.

"I'm not sure I'm physically or emotionally up to this assignment," I told my husband. "Besides, I don't know what I want to talk about."

"I'm sure you can do it," he replied, "and I know you'll think of something to say."

It went right down to the wire, but I did finally speak on the assigned topic. At the last minute, however, I decided to expand my talk and discuss the possibility of starting a prayer group and a healing ministry. I was well aware that I had been the focus of a mighty prayer effort because I was the pastor's wife. I knew what that kind of support meant to me, and I reasoned that any other sick member of our parish should also have access to it if prayer was needed or requested.

That Sunday the parish hall was filled for the adult forum. I suspected that some persons had come out of curiosity. St. John's is a parish of high calibre executive-type people—all chiefs, no Indians. They have opinions and they never hesitate to state them or to ask questions. Following my talk not one question was asked; no one ventured an opinion when I challenged them to consider prayer and healing as a part of our parish life. I could read the minds of some: "Poor Mary! She not only has cancer, she's also gone off the deep end." Some still think so.

I soon learned that the reason for the silence was that people hesitate to talk *publicly* about their belief in prayer and a healing Christ. One by one individuals came and confided that they believed prayer to be important and that they would join a prayer group. So we set a meeting date.

About ten people came to that first meeting. There we decided to visit St. Stephen's to learn what we could about prayer groups and the healing ministry. Dr. Price gave us a full morning of his time. Later we all attended a healing service. The experience was memorable. We resolved then and there to start healing services in our own parish.

I went through the official channels, first approaching the worship and music committee which then recommended such

6

services to the church council. The recommendation was approved. I'm sure the action was speedy because they wanted to "keep Mary happy" for as long as I would be around.

We decided to move right ahead and hold our first service in the middle of July. No fancy publicity was issued. There was only a note each week in the Sunday church bulletin. We had no idea whether anyone besides the prayer group itself would come.

On that hot, humid Sunday evening in July we held our first healing service—and had our first miracle!

Dale was a lovely young woman who was having serious mental problems. She had been under psychiatric care for almost three years. Things had gotten so bad that she would not even get out of bed unless directed to do so by her psychiatrist. Somehow her mother had persuaded her to come to our first healing service. Dale later described her experience in a letter:

> I went to the service the first night and what I felt there was amazing. Christ was everywhere, in everyone. You just knew it and felt it. For the first time I was ready to take away the barrier and let him help me. Join with me in prayers of great rejoicing and thanks for what I consider a miracle.

The following week Dale made her own decision to go to Boston to visit a girl friend. The week after that she took a job. The next time she walked into her psychiatrist's office he said, "Well, Dale, welcome back to the world."

From that time on we held regular weekly healing services. We saw marital problems resolved, occupational situations straightened out, drug problems healed, brokenness of every sort mended.

Our services continued for a year before there was any publicity about them. We did not seek publicity because we regarded our healing services as a normal function of the total worship program. Most of the people who attended were our own church members.

Then things suddenly changed. A reporter for the *Newark Star*

Ledger called my husband: "I've been getting your church bulletins regularly and I've wondered what these healing services are all about. Would it be O.K. if I attended one?" He came to our next healing service.

As a result of his visit, a story about our healing ministry appeared on the front page of his Sunday edition. Very early that morning—the moment the paper hit the newstands—the phone at church started ringing. The phone at home started ringing. The phones rang all day. People were inquiring about the time of service and asking for information. That evening our chapel, which seats forty persons, was quickly filled to overflowing. Worshippers had to take chairs out in the narthex. We were overwhelmed at the obvious need for personal prayer.

I then decided to write an article on the healing ministry and submit it to a church magazine to which we subscribe. "I doubt that they'll even consider printing it," I told my husband.

"Mary, you know that the age of miracles isn't over," he replied. "Wait and see. After all, the editors are interested in what's happening in the church."

They printed my article, and six hundred letters poured in from people who believe that Christ lives, loves, forgives, and heals. Most of them acknowledged that their healing, whether physical or mental, involved spiritual healing as well. When the chips are down people turn to the Lord, believing.

A second article was written and published in the same magazine. Again the response was overwhelming. Pastors wrote. Lay people wrote. I began to realize that I needed to study the subject further.

As I became better informed, I became more and more committed to Christ as healer. Invitations to speak were coming in. My husband and I began seeking ways and finding opportunities to generate interest in prayer and healing services. Gradually, it became clear that the story of my own healing had been only the beginning of what was to become a continuing adventure.

2. Man—A Totality

> And the Lord God formed man of the dust of the ground, and breathed into his nostrils the breath of life; and man became a living soul.
>
> Genesis 2:7 (KJV)

A number of years ago a science fiction movie depicted a group of scientists who were placed in a submarine which was then reduced in size and injected into the vein of an ill person. They traveled through the body seeking to ascertain the cause of the illness. In the course of their "fantastic voyage" they kept looking for the soul of the person.

They did not find it, of course, because man does not *have* a soul. Man *is* a soul—a person made up of body, mind, and spirit. To say it another way, my soul is the "all of me." And healing, in the Christian sense, means wholeness of body, mind, and spirit—"all of me." Martin Heinecken says:

In the biblical account of creation we are told that God formed man of dust and of the earth, and that he then breathed into his nostrils, and man became a living soul. This is usually interpreted to mean that God made a soul, which is the real person, and that he gave this soul a temporary home in a body, made of dust of the earth. But this is a false dualism or twoness. The Bible does speak of a twoness in man; it is the old, natural man and the new man in Christ. This is quite different from a dualism of mind and matter or body and soul. Man is a unity.*

In the healing ministry we constantly emphasize the totality of man in his need for healing. The various facets or aspects of the soul (body, mind, and spirit) are interdependent, and the illness of any one part can affect all the other parts. The mind can create a pain in the leg; an ulcer in the stomach can depress the mind; guilt can cause pain in the chest.

9

Dr. Price tells the story of a man who came regularly to his services of healing. One day, after the service, the man approached him and said, "You know, Dr. Price, this healing business isn't working. I have a terrible case of arthritis and I come every week but I'm not getting any better."

"Well, let's go into my study and talk about it," replied the priest.

As they talked, Dr. Price discovered that the man had an intense hatred for his brother. He suggested, "Before you come to the healing service next week, go and make peace with your brother."

The man looked at him for a moment and then responded, "If that's what it takes, I'll suffer!"

Here we see the interdependence of body, mind, and spirit. A *spiritual* problem affected the man's body and, undoubtedly, his mental health as well. He needed to heed Jesus' advice: "Make peace with your brother" (Matt. 5:24). A doctor might have treated the physical problem, but only the Great Physician could have healed the spiritual brokenness.

Jesus always dealt with the whole person. Sometime after he had healed the paralytic at the pool Jesus found him in the temple and warned him to stop sinning or something worse could happen (John 5:2-18). Jesus made it clear that he was concerned for the man both physically and spiritually.

The story of the woman taken in adultery is a story of healing. A prostitute, she surely was as sick spiritually as a person with cancer is sick physically. Jesus forgave her, told her to sin no more, and, in bringing her into a right relationship with himself, made her whole. Forgiveness (a spiritual act) turned her away from her prostitution (a physical act).

Several months ago I was visiting regularly with a young woman confined to a mental institution. On one of my visits she asked, "Would you do me a favor?"

"I'd be glad to, Karen," I said. "What would you like me to do?"

"Please pray for me," she begged.

Her problems came tumbling out. She had been carrying a feeling of guilt since childhood and, as the years went by, the guilt grew and grew until it consumed her mind like a malignant growth.

I told her, "Karen, this is something Jesus can take care of. He wants to forgive this sin of the past if you will let him."

"Oh, I believe that Jesus can forgive me," she replied, "but I can't forgive myself."

We did a lot of talking. Then we prayed. She soon saw that she was making herself bigger than God by not forgiving herself when God was willing to forgive her. If we believe that the Creator forgives us, then we must also forgive ourselves.

Karen was fortunate in having a Christian psychiatrist who knew that awareness of guilt and confession of guilt were steps one and two. Her pastor helped her with step three, the acceptance of forgiveness. Today Karen is a healed person through the supportive efforts and prayers of the body of Christ.

The Christian ought to be aware of the totality of his being and of the unity of his physical and emotional make-up. We express the interrelatedness of body, mind, and spirit every day: "he was scared stiff"; "he burns me up"; "she fainted from fright"; "she flushed with embarrassment"; "he's a pain in the neck". Even the ancients knew that "as a man thinketh in his heart, so is he."

Genevieve Parkhurst* pictures man as living in a three-story house. There is the Man on the Ground Floor who runs the house, the Partner in the Basement, and the Cherub in the Penthouse. Man's conscious self lives on the first floor. It is this self that thinks, reasons, plans, and wills. To keep this self presentable to others, this Man opens the door to the basement and shoves all the trash down there, all the things he doesn't want anyone to see.

Man's Partner, his subconscious, lives in the basement. Down there he has lots of empty rooms in which to store the trash.

Whenever the Man on the Ground Floor wants something recalled from the trash, the Partner in the Basement finds it and sends it up. This, obviously, can cause a multitude of problems.

I am reminded of a church sexton who, instead of disposing of the church's trash (boxes, twine, excelsior), would store it in the basement, assuring himself that someday it might be useful. When the fire chief made his annual inspection he was shocked to see such an accumulation of junk. The church received a letter a few days later: "If you don't get rid of the trash in the basement you are going to be in big trouble."

So it is. When we store up the trash of unforgiven guilt, envy, jealousy, greed, hatred, unhealed memories, and other dangerous material, we expose ourselves to spontaneous combustion in the basement of the soul (the "all of me") and we become sick.

On the top floor of this self is the Cherub in the Penthouse. He represents the conscience, from which we get our inspiration and aspiration. The Cherub, like the Partner in the Basement, accepts what the Man on the Ground Floor sends up to him. If the Cherub in the Penthouse is repeatedly denied, he is no longer able to make his voice heard by the Man on the Ground Floor, and trouble ensues.

Almost any day we can pick up a magazine or newspaper and read how stress or tension can make a person ill. In a recent study of two thousand executives the Life Extension Institute reported: "Tension is not caused by age, occupation, or job demands. Tension is clearly identified with the personality of the individual executive and stems from within the man rather than from outer forces of his living or environment."

Even cancer, obviously a physical illness, may eventually be traced to emotional causes. According to a recent book by Howard and Martha Lewis,* cancer researchers are beginning to suspect that a person's emotional make-up may affect not only the onset of disease, but also its growth rate. Though far from conclusive, mounting evidence suggests that only certain types of people are "cancer-prone."

12

In my file I have letters from a woman who has a recurring pain in the side. This pain comes and goes, almost on command. The doctors have assured her that there is no physical problem. She does have marital and family problems, however, and the pain in her side always coincides with domestic flare-ups. Evidently, she sends messages down to the Partner in the Basement every time a family incident occurs and, sure enough, the pain in the side is sent up from the subconscious.

We need to clean up these dirty closets! The Christian has a daily opportunity to do so. Jesus washes them clean with his forgiveness if we let him. If this seems simple, it is. Today more than ever we need to say, "Christ died for my sins"—and believe it! The Holy Spirit is the Power available for healing. We often keep him locked up, however, in one of those basement rooms. Fortunately, more and more Christians are becoming aware of this mighty Resource ever present to heal.

Men in the healing professions increasingly think in terms of the whole person. Their research and experience have convinced them of the close interrelationship of body, mind, and spirit.

A friend of mine who is a urologist says frankly, "When I was a young doctor I thought medicine was primarily a science. Now I know it is mostly an art." He treats not just the physical ailment, but the soul, the person made up of body, mind, and spirit. My own doctor limits his practice in order that he will have time to spend with his patients and in order that, as he puts it, "I can know *you*." He is concerned about the whole patient—the "all of me."

Rollo May tells of the powerlessness he felt as he lay in a hospital bed, the victim of tuberculosis:

> Not until I developed some "fight," some sense of personal responsibility for the fact that it was *I* who had the tuberculosis, an assertion of my own will to live, did I make lasting progress. I learned to listen to my body with an inner concentration like meditation, to get guidance as to when to exercise and when to rest. I learned that healing and cure were active processes in which I myself needed to participate.*

The awareness that he, Rollo May, was more than his physical body contributed to his recovery. Without that awareness he may never have recovered.

Emily Gardner Neal tells of a physician's record which showed the relationship between a patient's spiritual health and his speedy recovery:

> Dr. Graham Clark, noted eye surgeon of New York's Columbia Presbyterian Medical Center, had long noted what seemed to him a significant disparity in the speed of healing, post-operative pain, and the need for drugs among patients undergoing the same operation. The charts he subsequently compiled confirmed his observation; although the normal medical variation in healing is 18%, his meticulously drawn charts revealed that the differential between the fastest and the slowest healing in the same surgical procedure is 400%. Curious to discover why, Dr. Clark compared the record of the people in the same age group, equally divided as to sex. His conclusion, based on this study, was that the committed Christian who is loving, considerate of others, uncomplaining, and has his life centered in Christ, heals far more rapidly, with less pain and less need of drugs, than others.*

Thus, to be healthy or whole I must know, not that I *have* a soul, but that I *am* a soul. To be well I need health in body, mind, and spirit. Healing always refers to the whole person. Healing of the body is important but not all-important. It is of great worth but not of supreme worth. Healing ministry focuses on the body penultimately and on the soul (the "all of me") ultimately.

3. What is the Healing Ministry?

> When evening came, people brought to Jesus many
> who had demons in them. Jesus drove out the evil
> spirits with a word and healed all who were sick. He
> did this to make come true what the prophet Isaiah
> had said, "He himself took our illnesses and carried
> away our diseases."

Matt. 8:16-17

There is much misunderstanding about the healing ministry.
Therefore, it is important right at the outset to indicate what
spiritual healing is not.

Spiritual healing is not a substitute for the doctor. One of the
greatest instruments of healing is the doctor. His professional
skills, his medical knowledge and insights are invaluable. These
are God-given treasures to be used to the fullest. According to
scripture, God looked at his creation and declared it was good. To
reject doctors and medicine is to reject God's creation, thereby
denying the goodness of God.

Frequently, people ask me to pray that they will not need the
services of a doctor. An older woman once wrote to ask if I
would pray that she would not have to wear a contact lens
following cataract surgery. "It is such a nuisance," she wrote.

I wrote back telling her I could not do this. If the avenue of
healing which God had provided her included wearing a contact
lens, then she would have to learn to wear it.

"I wear two contact lenses," I wrote, "and I'm grateful for
them. With contact lenses my vision is perfect and it has been
worth the effort. I will pray that you will have the patience and
fortitude to work at wearing your contact lens and to thank God
that he has provided this avenue of healing."

In the healing ministry we avail ourselves of every avenue of
healing, including trained doctors and the Great Physician.

15

Spiritual healing is not Christian Science. Jesus accepted the reality of physical suffering and did something about it—he healed. There is no record of his having ever said, "Your problems are just in your head." Instead we are told again and again that he was filled with compassion and healed. Jesus knew suffering himself. Because of this he understands us, loves us, and heals us.

Spiritual healing is not just positive thinking. Certainly a positive attitude on the part of the sick person and those about him is important in healing. It can sometimes make the difference between living and dying. However, positive thinking does not save, and the healing ministry is involved with the salvation of the whole person. Spiritual healing includes a person's relationship to Jesus Christ.

Spiritual healing is not just relief from pain. We must guard against using the Lord as a hot-water bottle, taking him off the shelf when we hurt and putting him back on the shelf when the pain is gone.

A woman wrote me, "Are you still there? Last year you prayed for my sister's heart condition. She's been healed. Now I need you to pray for my brother." She went on to describe his condition.

Our prayer group had indeed prayed and the Lord had in fact healed her sister, but the woman had never let us know so we could give him thanks. More importantly, she had never let the Lord know either. She had put him back on the shelf until another pain came along.

Spiritual healing is not faith healing. "I'm not getting well because I don't have enough faith. I just know it." Often this is the lament of the sick person. How tragic! To make healing dependent on the quantity of faith is to turn faith into a "good work." Yet, seriously ill people often crucify themselves, blaming their lack of healing on the smallness of their faith. All we need is the faith of a grain of mustard seed which, as Jesus said, is the smallest of seeds (Matt. 17:20).

I know personally that coping with a serious illness can so

consume a person's resources that there is no strength left for trying to build faith. It is not the amount of my faith that heals. It is my faith in Christ that *he* can heal. Jesus said to the woman healed of the issue of blood, "Your faith has made you well" (Luke 8:43-48). Her faith in herself? No, her faith that Jesus could heal her.

When someone says to me, "I wish I had your faith," I respond, "You may have it. Go ahead and use it. We are all part of the body of Christ, and any faith I have is not mine to keep; it is yours to use."

I believe that I am alive today, not because of my faith, but because of the faith of the body of Christ that responded to my need. Christians pooled their faith in Christ and prayed for me, a sick member of the one body, that I would be healed—and I was healed.

The "faith healer" tarnishes the work of the healing ministry. People put their faith in him rather than in Christ. By this route some people undoubtedly experience a physical or mental healing, but they are not healed in spirit. They are not made whole in a faith relationship to Christ.

Spiritual healing is not spiritualism. Many tend to confuse the two. Anne White rightly observes: "Spiritualism heals with the supposed aid of human departed spirits, whereas divine healing calls only upon the Third Person of the Trinity, the Holy Spirit."*

Once, after I made this point during a presentation on the healing ministry, a Roman Catholic priest told me, "I'm so glad you spoke about divine healing as contrasted to spiritualism. I've been having a rash of spiritualism in my parish. In fact, just this past week a woman had a complete mental breakdown as a result of her involvement in spiritualism. Unfortunately, she isn't the first one."

If this is what the healing ministry of the church is *not*, what then *is* it?

17

HEALING

Healing ministry is known by many names. I prefer the term "divine healing" because it most nearly describes the healing ministry as I understand it. Divine healing is the love of God that heals a soul—the "all of me"—in body, mind, and spirit. To use another phrase from Anne White: "Divine Healing is more than 'getting well'; it is being made whole."*

Wholeness involves the relationship to Christ. A woman wrote me, "For the first time in my life I have accepted Christ and the cross." This witness came from a person with a cancer that had been diagnosed a year earlier as "incurable." Since then she had joined a prayer group and found a real anchor in her life as she was supported, sustained, and brought to an acceptance of Jesus as her Lord. Having found the greatest healing of all, she is now gradually experiencing physical healing as well. She works every day and leads a full and normal life.

Divine healing is God's way of dealing with a sick person in such a way as to provide wholeness. It is God's way of dealing with the underlying causes of illness—and they are many:

Hate. In my own case I wondered how I happened to develop cancer in just a brief six months. I had had my annual checkup in August and was in fine physical condition. By March I was in the hospital with cancer. What had happened in the interim?

As I reconstruct it, I had started hating someone, and a person cannot hate and stay healthy. I had been involved in a "sensitivity session" at which a young couple bitterly attacked and screamed at my husband and me. Since the people in the group were all Christians, I was stunned and shocked. I developed a growing dislike for this couple, a dislike that grew into hate.

In the weeks that followed I could not even get near them without hatred and revulsion welling up within me. Several times I actually became sick to my stomach. I was spiritually ill, and my body became sick as a result. All the wrong "juices" started to flow.

Once, after I had shared this experience publicly, someone in the audience said, "God punished you for your hate." Nonsense! I punished myself.

18

Guilt. A friend of mine had nursed her ailing mother for many years. The mother had developed a serious heart problem, became a terrible burden, and finally died.

Janet suddenly developed the same pain in the chest, indeed all the symptoms her mother had had. She actually fainted from pain at times. Yet the doctor could find no evidence of heart trouble. He suggested that she see a psychologist.

After several months of therapy, Janet discovered that over the years she had deeply resented the fact that her mother was such a burden and took so much of her time and strength. Janet had also kicked the resentment down into one of those "basement" rooms, reassuring herself with the fact that she loved her mother. After the mother died, Janet began to feel guilty about the resentment, and, in punishing herself for it, she assumed all the physical symptoms of her mother.

Once the guilt was brought to light Janet was able to ask forgiveness, receive it, and become whole again. She was sick physically, mentally, and spiritually; it was a sickness that involved the whole person.

Worry. Nancy is a chronic worrier. "Mary," she says, "the healing ministry is the thing that keeps me going. I attend healing services every Sunday evening to get my 'spiritual vitamins.' "

It all began when her husband deserted her years ago. Her brother, with whom she lived, was constantly bickering with her over small things. Her parents caused unending problems. She had been institutionalized for a mental breakdown. So, over the years, she had worried incessantly about herself and her children.

Then she started to attend healing services each Sunday. She took all her worries to the altar where she knelt and gave them to the healing Christ, receiving the assurance of his love and his continuing presence. As a result, she found the courage to move into her own home. Relationships with her parents and brother improved. The children have benefited. No longer is Nancy burdened with accumulated worries. She has her "basement" cleaned out every week by the healing Christ.

Fear. Fear can strike the most stalwart of us. John was mayor

19

of a growing northern industrial town and president of a utility company. He was looked upon as a leader and a man of strength—but he was afraid.

For the first time in his life, at the age of seventy-eight, John was hospitalized. The illness was not serious, but fear impeded his recovery. It caused shortness of breath and made his heart beat rapidly.

John wrote and asked for prayer. Over the months he was led to the healing Christ. John became aware of the power of the Holy Spirit within him and was helped to see his fear as nothing to be ashamed of but something to be faced.

In our neighborhood there are two cats, a black one and an orange one. Every time the orange one comes into the yard my son's big hound, Gus, chases her. She turns in fright and runs up the nearest tree where she stays for many hours because she is too afraid to come down. The black cat is afraid too, but when Gus runs toward her she faces him, arches her back, stands her hair on end, looks him in the eye, and quite deliberately starts walking toward him. Finally, *Gus* turns and runs.

Humans can take a lesson from these animals. When we face fear, when we walk to meet it with faith, fear itself will turn tail and run.

The need to forgive and be forgiven. At healing services I always pray silently that the Holy Spirit will lead me in the prayers I offer publicly. At one such service a man knelt before me at the altar rail and whispered, "God knows my problem." I prayed that the man would be healed "spiritually."

After the service he asked: "How did you know that that prayer was the one to pray for me? I am so in need of spiritual healing."

We talked for almost an hour. Finally he said, "What I am about to tell you I have never told to any other person. I've kept this to myself for years."

Out from the "basement" came his problem. Years ago he had made a promise to the Lord. He had also made a promise to

20

another human being. Because the two promises were contradictory, he had sprung a trap on himself. In fulfilling his promise to the fellow human being, he had broken his promise to the Lord. But, he reasoned, had he kept his promise to the Lord, he would have wronged his fellow man.

All these long years he had not forgiven the fellow human for making him keep his promise, and he had not accepted the forgiveness of God, who, as I pointed out to him, must be more aware of the dilemma than he.

There, standing in the nave of the church, that man forgave another human being, accepted forgiveness from God, and was healed of a brokenness which had drained his whole soul for many long years. He stood straight, smiled, and walked out a whole person.

The desire to remain sick. Many people don't want to be completely healed. To be healed would take from them the interest, attention, and service they receive from others. Their pedestals would be gone.

A man came week after week to our healing services wearing a neckbrace. He divulged to me that he had been to the Mayo Clinic, only to be told that they could find nothing physically wrong.

As the weeks went by, I learned that there had been a serious problem between him and a neighbor which resulted in the neighbor's being arrested and sent to jail for a short term. "I didn't want him to go to jail," he said. "Just to be punished a little." At the same time the man was having trouble with his daughter. Then, too, his position at work was threatened because of his temper. Added to all of this, he was jealous of the job his wife held, and the jealousy produced serious marital problems.

From his pastor I learned that most of the man's problems were of his own creation. His daughter really loved him, his employer thought he was an extremely talented person, and his wife desperately wanted to save the marriage. But he shunned all their efforts to cooperate. He quit going to church, rebuffed the

21

pastor, who was a personal friend, and refused the Sacrament of the Altar. And the more difficult and withdrawn he became, the stiffer his neck got. His story does not have a "*happy ending.*" Not everyone wants total healing. This man willed not to avail himself of opportunities for the healing of the whole person.

Loneliness. A retired schoolteacher wrote: "I had surgery for a tumor some months ago. I recovered from the surgery but seem unable to gain weight and strength." As I read on I discovered the *real* problem: "I am seventy-two years old and live alone. My husband is dead. I have no children. My family lives a long way from here and sometimes I get very lonely."

This woman is one of those "lonely people" about whom the Beatles sang. There are so many of them one wonders where they all come from. Loneliness means brokenness, and brokenness needs healing. Each of us can bring healing to some lonely person. Everyone needs to be needed.

Among my correspondents is a widow who refuses to go into the hospital because she has three dogs. "They love me and need me," she writes. Her doctor feels she would be better off being hospitalized but, "There I would be just a patient in a bed. Here at home I'm a person who is needed and loved, even if it's only the dogs who need me and give me that love."

Recently I read about a dog named Laramie, a golden retriever that lives in a children's ward at a mental health center in Columbia, Missouri. Dr. Harry Hull, the ward psychiatrist, says, "For many of the children Laramie fills the human need for love."

What an indictment of the church when old people and children have to turn to dogs for companionship and love! Surely the body of Christ ought to be able to ward off loneliness.

Depression. Depression is not just a problem of older people. A young woman who was an adopted child reached the point in her life where she began to ask, "Who am I? Where did I come from? Why did my mother give me up?" She became exceedingly depressed over not knowing, and the result was a mental breakdown.

22

She sent for the pastor and requested anointing and laying-on-of-hands. She is now a healed person, knowing the most important truth there is to know and accept—that she is God's child.

Hate, guilt, worry, fear, the need to forgive and be forgiven, the desire to remain sick, loneliness, depression—all of these and more must be considered as possible underlying causes of illness. "Why am I sick?" This is a natural and frequently posed question. The lament usually runs something like this: "I am a good person. I have always attended church regularly and communed frequently. I have taught Sunday School and sung in the choir. Why has this happened to me?"

Jesus gave an answer to the question when he said of the woman bent double for eighteen years, "Satan hath bound her" (Luke 13:10-17). Jesus did not blame God.

Referring to his thorn in the flesh, Paul did not say, "God gave me this." Rather, he spoke of his problem as a "messenger from Satan to buffet me" (2 Cor. 12:7).

Not only Satan, but man himself brings brokenness and illness upon himself. Countless thousands of us need healing as a result of our disobedience in not loving our neighbor. Man has made war, wreaked destruction, decimated bodies, and fostered starvation, disease, and disorder within and among nations.

Our Heavenly Father is not an American citizen. He is not a tribal God dedicated to the American way of life. He loves all people and all nations. He longs for healing among all peoples and reconciliation with himself. His son died for all. When we fail to love all—even our enemies—we are disobedient children and bring brokenness upon ourselves and others.

For Christians, healing is not a special ministry. It is a way of life—love's way. It is not just a matter of intensive praying and attending extra services. It is part and parcel of being, as Luther put it, a "little Christ" to my neighbor—at every moment ready to forgive and be forgiven, and to offer assurance, hope, and friendship.

Through love and prayer the Christian can bring that unique

23

kind of healing which is not the professional responsibility of the doctor, the psychologist, or the psychiatrist. While doctors "practice" the church prays. Doctors are honest enough to admit that they "practice" on the patient! Only the church prays with and for the patient. As it is the doctor's business to practice medicine, it is the church's business to pray to God. And it is God's business to heal.

Paul Tillich speaks of the responsibility to bring healing when he says:

> Everyone is potentially a tool of healing for anyone else. The fact that Jesus gave the disciples responsibility for healing and casting out demons does not constitute a special prerogative on the part of the minister. Every Christian received this charge, and each of us should take it seriously in our relation to one another. Everyone should accept his priestly responsibility for everyone else.*

To bring healing means to love, and love compels action. Thus, healing means giving of self and loving the unlovable. Emily Gardner Neal muses:

> If one were to search for the single attribute most characteristic of the healing ministry, I suspect that he would find it is love. Saying this is not to imply that Christian love is restricted to the ministry of healing, but only to affirm that love is present to an uncommon degree in people who are involved in any way with this ministry, whether they actively work in it, participate regularly in healing services as supplicants, or just believe in the healing Christ.*

As a seventeen year old lad once expressed it to my husband following a healing service, "There's something different about the healing service, something I can feel there that I don't feel at the regular Sunday morning service. I think it's love."

24

4. What is a Healing Service?

> Is there any one of you who is sick. He should call the
> church elders, who will pray for him and pour oil on
> him in the name of the Lord. This prayer, made in
> faith, will save the sick man: the Lord will restore him
> to health, and the sins he has committed will be for-
> given. Therefore, confess your sins to one another, and
> pray for one another, so that you will be healed.
>
> James 5:14-16

A healing service is a service held for the sole purpose of
ministering to, and praying with and for, individual persons who
desire healing in body, mind, and spirit for themselves or others.

People sometimes wonder about the need for such separate
services. Pastors particularly, but laymen as well, often feel that
every personal need is met in the normal Sunday morning
worship service. There scripture is read, the Word is preached,
confession is made, absolution is pronounced, prayer is offered,
and the sacraments are administered.

Yet for some individuals, the sick especially, a more personal
approach is sometimes needed. There are certain times in their
lives when they feel the need for a special service where people
can come together with singleness of purpose and express their
concern for healing.

On a Sunday morning the people attending church bring a
variety of expectations. They come to hear the sermon, to enjoy
the choir, to partake of the sacrament, to praise God—or just
because it's Sunday and that's the thing they always do on
Sunday. It would be naive to say that a congregation assembled
for worship on any given Sunday morning is single-mindedly
pursuing a common goal. The singular focus of the healing service
allows the worshippers a greater community of mind and purpose.

A healing service, as we conduct it, in form is quite similar to the morning service, except that the individuals attending have the opportunity to be ministered to on a one-to-one basis. Focused specifically on the healing of persons, such a service includes the following elements:

Reading from scripture. The Bible abounds with the promises of God. It is impossible to read or hear these promises too often. Even now, as I read the Bible, I come upon passages that leap out at me and speak to me, and I wonder how I could have read them so often before without having ever grasped their meaning. As Christians we need constantly to hear the Word of God. More often than not the scripture for a healing service is identical to the lessons used that same day in the regular Sunday service.

Confession of sins. In my own church we have public confession each week. We corporately confess that we have "sinned in thought, word, and deed." For some people, though, this general confession is not enough. They need to say what the specific thought, word, or deed is. And they need to say openly before another Christian. In our healing missions people are given the opportunity, as they kneel at the altar rail, to say why they are there. Where a healing service is being held for the first time, the pastor usually expects that his people will not want to verbalize their desires. And he is usually surprised, for nine out of ten persons do articulate their needs. In many instances the need is for confession. Often this is the first time that worshippers have been given an opportunity to confess their sin to another person. Yet to do so is a basic human need.

Forgiveness of sins and absolution. We all need to be assured of forgiveness. As individual members of the body of Christ on earth we need also to forgive each other. In the healing service we do just that. We forgive each other. Then we turn in prayer to ask the Lord's forgiveness. And we assure the penitent personally that he is absolved of all sin by the power of the risen Christ.

Preaching of the gospel. The gospel is always preached at a healing service. Whenever my husband preaches, for example, he takes his text from one of the appointed lessons for the day. Since healing involves the whole person (the "all of me") the gospel can always be applied to some facet of the person's life that is in need of healing. This is one point at which the healing service differs from the regular Sunday morning service; the sermon always relates to some aspect of healing—the healing of body, mind, or spirit, and of relationships, both personal and corporate.

Anointing and laying-on-of-hands. We follow the directive of James in using oil to anoint the sick. We simply make the sign of the cross on the person's forehead and say, "I anoint you with oil in the name of the Father, and of the Son, and of the Holy Spirit."

Just as we can receive forgiveness without bread and wine, so we can receive healing without oil. As human beings, however, we often find visible signs helpful. Thus, we use oil in our service merely as a visible and external sign.

Also, several members of the body of Christ (often a pastor and a layman) lay hands on the head of the one kneeling at the altar rail. Jesus touched many of those who came to him for healing. We too need the human touch. It conveys love. If my husband said that he loved me, yet never touched me, I would have real doubt about that love. The person who is ill needs to have love demonstrated as well as spoken. A compassionate touch from the body of Christ conveys the love of God in a very personal way.

Prayers for the sick. After a person has knelt, been anointed, and stated his prayer request, he is prayed for personally. For some this is the first time in their lives that they have had a personal prayer said aloud on their behalf before God's altar and in their presence.

These prayers are usually short and to the point. Jesus advises us: "In your prayers do not use lots of words, as the pagans do, who think that God will hear them because they use a lot of words. Do not be like them: your Father already knows what

27

you need before you ask him" (Matt. 6:7-8). Jesus said this just before giving us the Lord's Prayer, a model of brevity as well as completeness in prayer.

Opportunity for counseling. It is important that the pastor and concerned laymen be available both before and after the healing service. Many times people will want to talk to someone about their problems. That opportunity must be provided—sometimes obviously, at other times more subtly. To be a counselor means to be a listener. People have said to me, "You've been such a help with my problem." Maybe so. Yet all I've done is listen. As a part of counseling I always have a prayer with an individual once his story is told. But I never tell him what he should do. I listen, actively.

The healing service can be private. Christians normally receive Holy Communion of their own volition at a public service. But if they cannot come, because of illness for example, they request that the sacrament be brought to them where they are. Likewise people come to a healing service because they decide to do so. But if they cannot come, perhaps because of confining illness, the service can, upon request, be brought to them.

A private service in home or hospital should be brief. Remember, the person is sick, Nonetheless, a few introductory words should be said to help the patient understand that no magic is going to take place and that the role of his doctor is not to be compromised.

Naomi was desperately sick when she sent word from the hospital that she wanted a healing service. A collapse of the circulatory system had taken place. Two operations were performed. At first it was thought that she would not live. Later it was feared that she would lose a leg.

The service she requested was held right there in the hospital. She lived. And she still has two legs. No one can convince Naomi that she would be here today without the presence of the healing Christ which was assured her in that healing service. Coincidence? "All I know is that when I stop praying, the coincidences stop happening!"*

28

Healing services can be preventive medicine. They help to keep a person well. In a presentation to a group of pastors and their wives, Granger Westberg told of his experience in bringing doctors and clergy into closer relationship. A clinic was set up in which every patient was required to see both a doctor and a minister or priest. That way the whole person was treated. The cooperative effort was almost too successful; the hospital that served the area started to have empty beds—and those beds needed to be filled if the hospital were to get money from the federal government. "Imagine that you are the patient next in line when a doctor suddenly realizes that he has to fill beds," said Westberg. "You quickly find yourself between the sheets in a short nightie, and in all probability, since you are in a hospital, you will decide to be as sick as you are made out to be."

I have often thought that insurance companies would do well to establish foundations for training persons (laity and clergy) in the healing ministry. The preventive medicine would pay for itself in reduced hospitalization benefits.

The back cover of a church bulletin for St. Luke the Evangelist Day declared, "Healing is something more than what happens in hospitals. A concern for healing carries us still further. It leads us to be part of a 'preventive medicine' ministry."*

Just as doctors can vaccinate against disease, so the church can immunize against dis-ease. The church can thereby provide preventive medicine in the realm of the spirit.

What is accomplished more readily at a healing service than at a regular worship service? Eight unique opportunities are offered in a healing service.

First, there is the opportunity for personal confession. When a person comes to the altar and feels the need to confess his sin (remember, this is a spiritual sickness) he finds it necessary to capsulize his problem in a few short sentences; there is no time for a long dialogue, for hedging, for playing psychological games. In a counseling situation it may take hours before a person is able to articulate his problem. At the altar he comes right out with it.

I recall one service at which a couple knelt before the pastor and me, and the woman looked up with tears in her eyes to say, "We would like to ask Jesus to help us save our marriage."

The pastor was visibly shaken. These parishioners were also close friends. A number of us had been with them at dinner only the night before, and there was no apparent problem. Yet, at God's altar, they had grasped the opportunity to say to the risen Christ what they could not say to the pastor personally.

Second, in the context of a healing service there is the opportunity for personal witness. The Bible is a continuous record of man's encounter with God and a witness of that encounter. We still need this person-to-person witness today. Ideally, a healing service should provide an opportunity for personal witness, not only because people need it, but also because faith generates faith. A personal witness can engender hope, and hope can make the difference between living and dying.

After speaking to a group of Christians in my hometown, a young woman said with great emotion, "I have been praying for an opportunity like this." Then she shared her witness, a witness to God's healing her of cancer. It was the first time she had been able to make a witness to a group of gathered Christians. It did something for her *and* for the group.

Jesus sent the messengers back to John saying, "Go back and tell John what you are hearing and seeing: the blind can see, the lame can walk, the lepers are made clean, the deaf hear" (Matt. 1:4-6). We, too, must go and tell. A healing service provides a vehicle to do so.

A healing service provides, in the third place, an opportunity for each person to be anointed with oil. The writer of James advises the use of oil in healing (James 5:14-16). And the writer of Mark indicates the disciples anointed the sick with oil (Mark 6:13). The Old Testament indicates that anointing was a common practice among the Israelites. "Thou anointest my head with oil" (Ps. 23:5) is a verse familiar to us all. As Morton Kelsey says:

30

Although it is not stated that Jesus used oil in healing, the probability is that he did. This was certainly a common healing practice from the earliest times in the history of the church, and has continued uninterrupted in Eastern orthodox tradition.*

The Roman Catholic Church long connected an ominous meaning with the sacrament of extreme unction; the patient was as good as dead. Only recently Pope Paul VI changed all that. Since Vatican II the rite has been vested with new meaning as the "anointing of the sick." It is used for sick people and has no connotations about terminal illness. Father Secondo Mazzarello, a liturgical expert, comments: "The aim is now to comfort the sick person. Pain and sickness are seen as the problem of the entire man, body and soul together. The new rite gets away from the Platonic concept which for centuries split man into body and soul."*

A healing service can take place, of course, whether or not anointing is part of it. But anointing, whether viewed as a sacrament or not, has a venerable tradition in the church.

Fourth, the opportunity is given for laying-on-of-hands. Jesus and the disciples used this method almost instinctively. There are many instances of the use of the touch recorded in scripture: Jesus touched the blind man twice (Mark 8:23), he touched Peter's mother-in-law (Matt. 8:5), he touched Jairus's daughter (Matt. 9:25), and believers were directed to lay hands on the sick (Mark 16:17-28).

Human beings need to be touched. Last year my daughter, who teaches sixth grade, had a boy in her class who came and stood close to her at the beginning of each day. She either draped her arm around him or laid her hand on his shoulder, just briefly; then he'd run off, happy. Materially, this child had everything, but his parents were so heavily involved outside the home that their child needed his teacher's touch.

During a recent radio interview the president of the Jewish War Veterans, who had just returned from Russia, told of

31

speaking in a synagogue there. At the close of his talk he offered to answer questions—but there were no questions, because of fear. However, as he walked down the aisle after the meeting, people reached out and touched him. "Their touch," he declared, "said more to me than a thousand words."

The healing love of Christ can flow through the hands of the body of Christ. Martin Luther, on June 1, 1545, wrote a letter to a pastor who had asked for his help in dealing with a mentally ill person. Among other things, Luther advised the pastor to take a deacon or two or three good men, go to the man, lay hands on him, and pray for him. Obviously, Luther realized the value of the touch.

Fifth, the opportunity is given for personal prayer in a healing service. The scripture enjoins us to "pray for one another." We use laymen as well as pastors to do just that. Pastors are also prayed for by their people. How many times have you heard a pastor prayed for, publicly and personally, by a member of his parish? A healing service opens up the possibility.

A healing service, in the sixth place, gives an opportunity for personal assurance of forgiveness. A pastor pronouncing a blanket absolution to a congregation is sufficient for most people, but there are always some people who need a more personal assurance of forgiveness.

The secretary of a local official had been asked to do something she knew to be illegal and dishonest. She refused and lost her job. Bitterness and resentment were consuming her. She came to the altar saying, "I need to forgive and be forgiven." And there, in a meaningful moment, she told the whole story.

This woman was a faithful churchgoer. She communed regularly. Yet she needed someone to assure her personally that she was forgiven. She confessed, forgave, and accepted forgiveness. Her profound change in attitude was noticeable. She regained her charm and pleasantness and finally secured a better position than the one she had lost. In her case the normal Sunday morning service did not fill her need for personal forgiveness.

Seventh, a healing service also gives the opportunity for personal counseling. True, the pastor is available for counseling at all times. But many times the lay people of the parish can also be effective and able counselors as he. Pastors should not hesitate to let their members function as "little Christs" to their neighbors in need.

Dale, the young woman from our former parish who had recovered from a mental illness, was quite adept in relating to members of her peer group who had problems similar to her own. She was most helpful to two distraught parents who started coming to our healing services with their twenty-three year old son. While they lingered after the service to talk, he would go stand in a corner, alone. He had severe mental depression but refused to see a doctor. Dale started to sit with this young man during the healing service, go to the altar with him, kneel with him, and then pray for him. She talked to him and told him of her own struggles with mental illness. Finally, she persuaded him to admit himself to a nearby hospital where he could get psychiatric help. During his confinement the church and the doctor pooled their special abilities for making the young man whole. That's the healing ministry at work.

On another occasion two mothers were introduced to each other at the end of a service. One had a daughter who had been through the drug scene and was recovering. The other had a daughter who was still deeply involved with drugs. The first mother could counsel and support the other—and she did. She knew far more than the pastor about this problem. That's the healing ministry at work.

A man came to the pastor's study prior to a healing service. He had lost his job as a stock analyst on Wall Street and was literally "sick" about it. Unable to secure a similar job with a different firm, he thought he was being unfairly treated. The body of Christ was allowed to function when the pastor put him in touch with another man in the parish who was knowledgeable in the same field. In a short time the man had a new job, his confidence was restored, and he was a different person. That's the healing ministry at work.

Finally, the healing service offers an opportunity for nurturing a person's hope. People who attend healing services are either looking for hope or hoping to impart it, for hope is central to healing. Harold Wolff, research scientist in psychosomatic medicine, has written, "Hope, like faith and a purpose in life, is medicinal. This is not merely a statement of belief, but a conclusion proved by meticulously controlled scientific experiment."*

More than once I have been asked, "Isn't there the danger of giving false hope?"—meaning, "What if the person prayed for dies or is not healed according to his personal desire?"

Ultimate healing takes place only at the resurrection, when the new man arises to live with Christ face to face. Most Christians understand and accept this. We are not shattered if the person prayed for dies. Christians do not weep as others who have no hope. Precisely because we are Christians, though, what we want is for him to die healthy—a person made whole in body, mind, and spirit by the healing Christ.

Our prayer group was praying intensely for a man hospitalized by a coronary attack. His wife had called to say that he was in a coma and that the doctor felt there was no hope of his regaining consciousness. Death was expected within a matter of hours at most. Each member of the group was contacted by phone and we all prayed. The stricken man lived until the next day. He came out of his coma just long enough to look at his wife and say, "Carla, I love you." Then he died and experienced ultimate healing.

Carla rejoiced over that final moment and that last expression of love. "I have those words to keep with me until we meet again." She is sure that the prayer group helped to give her that last rich moment. She had, of course, hoped for his physical recovery. But her hope also went beyond that to embrace the assurance of a reunion with her husband in the resurrection.

These are some of the distinctive opportunities afforded by the healing service. A service of this kind emphasizes the peculiarly personal—and eternal—concern of the healing Christ for the members of his body, the church.

5. What Can I do to be Healed?

Jesus was coming near Jericho, and a certain blind man was sitting and begging by the road. When he heard the crowd passing by he asked, "What is this?" "Jesus of Nazareth is passing by," they told him. He cried out, "Jesus, Son of David! Have mercy on me!" The people in front scolded him and told him to be quiet. But he shouted even more loudly, "Son of David! Have mercy on me!" So Jesus stopped and ordered that the blind man be brought to him. When he came near, Jesus asked him, "What do you want me to do for you?" "Sir," he answered, "I want to see again." Then Jesus said to him, "See! Your faith has made you well." At once he was able to see, and he followed Jesus, giving thanks to God.

Luke 18:35-43

Most sick people sooner or later ask the question, "What can I do to be healed?" The story of the blind man on the road to Jericho suggests that healing is the gift and action of the Lord alone. However, it also offers clues as to the nature of man's involvement in his own healing. What did the blind man do?

As the story begins, he was sitting and begging. But he was listening too, because he heard the crowd passing by. He asked what was happening and learned that Jesus was also passing by. Then he took action; he cried out to Jesus. He refused to be put off by the crowd's attempt to quiet him. He continued to cry out, asked for mercy, allowed himself to be taken to Jesus, listened to Jesus' questions, answered them, and received in faith the gift that was offered. Having seen Jesus, he followed him and gave thanks. All this the blind man *did*.

Like this man, we can participate in the action of God that effects our own healing. There are things we can do that will be conducive to healing by the Great Physician, healing of the whole

36

person—body, mind, and spirit—through medical and other means of his own choosing.

The suggestions listed here are not exhaustive. However, they have been helpful to me and to others I know.

Search the scriptures. We hear the Word of God read regularly in church, but we should also read it for ourselves. It is helpful to examine the New Testament stories of healing for passages which relate to one's own situation. I underline every passage I find which has to do with healing. And the more I read the more I find.

Good books on healing also provide hope and inspiration. Often they are written by persons who have had unforgettable experiences with the healing Christ. These writers may present a variety of interpretations and approaches but they all agree on the power of Christ as healer.

Receive Holy Communion regularly. One of the finest healing services a person can experience is that of Holy Communion. In the sacrament Christ comes in a personal way in order that we might have the more abundant life. As Emily Gardner Neal puts it:

> He is always present and accessible, but in Holy Communion we enter into a unique relationship with Him, a union not possible for many of us in any other way. Receiving His body and blood we are fused with Him and infused by Him. We take into ourselves His Life, not only His Grace.*

A close friend of mine thought I might wonder why she never attended a healing service. "Mary," she said, "I find everything I need in the Sacrament of the Altar." I know she does and I thank God for that.

A contemporary liturgy includes this prayer at the point where the bread and wine are consecrated:

> Send the power of your Holy Spirit upon us and upon this bread and wine; that we who receive the body and blood of Christ may be

his body in the world, living according to his example to bring peace and healing to all mankind.*

In receiving the Holy Communion we are actually asking the Holy Spirit to involve us, as the body of Christ, in the healing of all mankind.

John Sutherland Bonnell once had an extraordinary experience in administering the sacrament. He tells of a close friendship he had had over many years with a physician. When the two of them got together they frequently celebrated the Sacramental Meal as a rite of friendship and faith. They always used three glasses—one for each participant and one for the Unseen Guest.

In later years the physician suffered a cerebral hemorrhage and his condition deteriorated rapidly. He did not recognize his friend or even his own family. When Dr. Bonnell went to visit the man he set before him the usual three glasses, the wine, and the wafers—a reminder to the doctor that Christ was present now as he had always been before. The service of Holy Communion was read aloud with the old gentleman coming in on the amens. Slowly recollection was restored and they shared a period of rational remembrance and fellowship. A Power was present that transcended even age and disease. Dr. Bonnell says it was one of the most dramatic experiences he has ever had.*

We live in a constant state of need to receive the sacrament, to experience its healing power. For me personally the need is to come to the table of the Lord regularly, each week if possible.

Attend healing services regularly. If services of healing are available to you and you benefit from attending them, then by all means go regularly. Faith can thereby be strengthened. We go to our medical doctors, not only when we need treatment, but for regular checkups as well. Certainly we should seek out the Great Physician with the same faithfulness.

A delightful old couple who come faithfully to our healing services are quick to tell anyone who will listen that they have experienced healing and that they continue to be sustained by their weekly attendance. We all love them and they know it. When we "pass the peace" among the worshippers, this couple is always hugged and kissed in genuine Christian love by the people about them. He says simply, "We need this service." Several years ago she had had a heart seizure while attending a healing service. Someone commented, "Isn't that something? She attends a healing service and gets sicker instead." His answer: "Weren't we fortunate that it happened when it did, while all those people were there and could pray for her? No wonder she experienced healing!"

Become a part of a prayer group. The support a sick person receives from being an integral part of a prayer circle is invaluable. Each member of the circle knows the other members personally, and they are always available for support and help when the going gets rough. It is true, where two or three are gathered in his name Christ is in their midst and his power is felt.

Recently one of our members, a rather quiet person, sought the support of the group: "Tonight I want to share some of my fears and anxieties." She went on to do just that—clearly, honestly, openly. As she spoke the whole group was with her, supporting her, and our final prayer that evening was offered on her behalf. Prayers for her were also uttered daily in many prayer closets.

Be persistent. "Be persistent in prayer, and keep alert as you pray, with thanks to God" (Col. 4:2).

Persistence brings results. For over two years I have been in correspondence with a man who was filled with fears and doubts. Despite the attendant physical problems, real and imagined, he persevered and, as of this writing, is happy, content, and well. Over these many months it would have been easy for him at any time to give up. But he did not, and now as I reread his letters I can see how he has gradually grown healthy in body and mind and also in spirit. Healing is not always instantaneous. But persistence in prayer does pay off. A broken person can grow into a mended and whole person, strengthened in his relationship to Christ as Lord.

"Practice the presence." Until the time of my illness I had never been aware of Christ's daily presence in my life. On my tedious path to recovery, however, I could do little but sit, and read, and think, and pray, and—for the first time—really look at a drop of dew on a blade of grass and feel the presence of the Creator. It was then that I learned to talk to him constantly— anywhere, anytime. Oh, I had always had my appointed time of prayer, but I was not conscious at all times of his nearness. Now, as I talk to people, I have an "Instant Consultant" to strengthen and guide me.

While I believe that everyone should consciously try to be aware of Christ's presence, it is especially helpful to people who are not well. There is strength and power in the feel of his presence. Work at it until it becomes an integral part of your total consciousness.

Pray for others. Does this seem like strange advice for a person who is ill? Actually, sick people can be powerful pray-ers. They are more aware of the need for prayer and of the power inherent in it. They are also more willing to dedicate themselves to the task of daily intercession.

To pray for another is to switch one's attention away from one's self and to concentrate on the needs of others. One allows oneself to be used as a channel through which the healing love of Christ can flow to another—to the benefit of both.

A friend in Michigan frequently is a patient in the hospital. There she always finds another patient for whom she can pray. She says, "I always discover that someone in that hospital needs me at that particular time to support him and pray for him. It is the Holy Spirit's way of getting me to where I am needed."

Have patience. I am not by nature a patient person. It took quite awhile for me to learn that "you need to be patient, in order to do the will of God and receive what he promises" (Heb. 10:36). Recovery for me was a gradual process; it gave me time to grow spiritually and, in the growing, to learn God's will for me. Had I not been ill, I might never have considered the healing ministry as a life commitment.

40

The man who reads our water meter stopped one day to chat about his recent surgery. "I didn't want the operation," he said, "but it was an experience I wouldn't have wanted to miss. I learned so much, and the first thing I did when I got home was to give assurance to my neighbor who was facing the same surgery. I didn't think I would have the patience to put up with this kind of thing, but it's really been a blessing to me in the lessons I've learned."

Give health to others by way of praise and approval. Remember the story of Robert and Elizabeth Browning? Until she was almost forty years of age she was a sofa-bound invalid ruled by a tyrannical father. Then Robert Browning came into her life. He gave her love and hope. He helped to overcome her fears. And finally he married her. She traveled extensively at the age of forty-one, had a child at the age of forty-three, and became a highly acclaimed poet. One person giving encouragement and love can change another that much.

A kind word can make someone's day better and happier. We all have the capacity—indeed, the responsibility—to bring health by being a "little Christ" to our neighbors.

Trust your doctor. Go to him regularly, but also pray for him. Use every channel of healing the Lord provides, including medicine and medical doctors. Pray that God will bless and use all his servants, all those who attend us in times of illness.

My husband and his surgeon talked recently about the dimension of man beyond the doctor's scalpel. Among other things, the surgeon said, "When I have a patient who says he will pray for me, I know that I will have more confidence in my abilities and that the patient will heal faster."

A personal friend who is also a pediatrician and cancer specialist tells me that families who have faith cope with their children's leukemia better than families without faith. Where faith is evident the doctor too is helped and encouraged, because she knows there will be fewer problems both physically and emotionally.

Confess your sins. "Happy is the man whose sins are forgiven" (Ps. 32:1). The responsible person knows when he has sinned, he

41

knows the need of forgiveness, and he knows he must confess in order to receive forgiveness. He knows that God is always willing to forgive whether man confesses or not, but that knowledge does not remove the guilt. Only confession does that. Forgiveness is like a gift that is ready and waiting, but can be possessed only as the person reaches out and receives it. In the act of confession we reach out for the gift that makes us whole. Peter Ford, the psychiatrist and surgeon, writes:

> It seems to me that modern psychiatry offers no definitive solution for the dilemma of human guilt, for neither punishment, modification of the superego, nor any form of denial, repression or rationalization will ever eradicate guilt. While it may temporarily diminish it, it never removes it. Forgiveness alone provides the only permanent resolution for guilt.*

Expect the miracle. Scripture is full of individuals who acted expectantly. When Eli, the priest, assured Hannah that God had heard her earnest petition and would grant her what she had so long desired—a child to bring an end to her barrenness—she did not just sit around to see what would happen. No! She promptly put on a happy face, ended her fast, and waited expectantly for the baby she would eventually name Samuel (I Sam. 1:18). When the Roman officer was told that his sick servant would be healed, he did not sit around in puzzled bewilderment or wait for someone to bring him word from home. No! He went home, as Jesus had told him to do, and found his servant healed (John 4:50). When Jesus told the paralyzed man to pick up his bed and go home, the man did not say, "Wait until I see if I can move." No! He got up, picked up his bed, and went home praising God (Luke 5:25). In each of these cases there was active expectancy, not passive unresponsiveness.

Possibly nothing hinders healing more than doubt within the body of Christ. When the honest doctor says, "I have done all I can," many families start making funeral arrangements. Believe me, the patient senses this. From experience, I know that attitudes speak louder than words to a sick person. More than once, while I was hospitalized and convalescing, it was I who cheered up my callers when I caught the message of gloom they inadvertently conveyed to me.

In healing we need to be active participants who respond in faith to the healing Christ. If you come expecting nothing to happen, nothing will happen. An expectant attitude, a positive and active faith, is necessary to the healing process.

Doubt effectively blocks the channel through which God's healing love can flow. Even Christians can hinder or stop the flow of healing power.

A young man in a parish I was visiting had been told that he had terminal cancer. The local prayer group had been asked to pray for him. Everyone I met said, "Isn't it sad? Carl isn't going to live." A solid wall of doubt, deep and impenetrable, had been built around this young man. It had been built by his fellow Christians. Malcolm Miner insists:

> When doubt and fear find their way into the picture a dark cloud hovers over the sickroom and that gloom infects the people who surround the patient—the nurses, the family members and close friends—and the patient himself.*

If we placed half as much confidence in the Great Physician as we do in our doctors, miracles would happen. But we seldom give the Lord a chance.

"People do die," you may say. And that's true. Surely they must die from something. But why can't a person die healthy? Surely we have all heard of persons who were here one minute and with the Lord the next. They moved from earth to heaven as easily as walking from the house to the garden, without any suffering at all.

43

6. The Body of Christ and Healing

> And so there is no division in the body, but all its
> different parts have the same concern for one another.
> If one part of the body suffers, all the other parts
> suffer with it; if one part is praised, all the other parts
> share its happiness. All of you, then, are Christ's body,
> and each one is a part of it.
>
> 1 Cor. 12:25-27

Prior to my illness I had never thought about how much I
depend on the rest of the body of Christ. During that illness,
however, when I was so exhausted coping with physical problems
that I had no reserve energy left for trying to strengthen my faith,
I was blessed as the body of Christ responded to my need. I am
positive that I live today because of that response—an entire
congregation praying for me at a special service of healing, at the
regular Sunday service, and at the morning prayer services which
were a daily part of the congregation's life.

As a member of the body, I now have the responsibility to
come to the aid of any other member and, if I am to be helpful,
to keep myself as healthy as I can in body, mind, and spirit. I
must daily drown the "old Adam" and allow the "new man in
Christ" to arise. As Bishop Eivind Berggrav said, "The reason we
must drown the 'old Adam' daily is because we wake up each
morning and find the old boy can swim." Healing is a continuing
process. If the whole body is to be healthy, each individual
member needs to seek daily the healing of the spirit.

The question is often asked, "Can I request prayer for someone else?" The obvious answer is "yes." Indeed, the most
important thing one member of Christ's body can do for another
member may be to intercede on his behalf. An intercessor is one
who prays for another. This praying can be done anywhere,
anytime—in one's own prayer closet or at a public service.

In healing services I find that most people actually come to the altar rail as intercessors, approaching God on behalf of someone else—even as the centurion came to Christ for his son (Matt. 8:5-23), a mother came for her daughter (Matt. 15:2-28), and a father came for his son (John 4:46-54).

Paul admonishes us to bear each other's burdens (Gal. 6:23). James tells us to pray for one another (Jas. 5:16). As a member of the body, each of us needs to pray for others—and to be prayed for by others.

The story is told of a great cathedral preacher who had people thronging to the services each week to hear him preach. Every Sunday a brother in his order would stand behind one of the great pillars of the nave, out of sight, and pray that the great man would be led by the Spirit in all that he said. A Sunday came when the great preacher stood in his pulpit as usual, but the words refused to come. He faltered at numerous points and the sermon just did not go well at all. Realizing his dependence upon his brother's intercessions, he sought out the brother right after the service. He went directly to the kitchen, where the brother was supposed to be washing pots, but the man was not there. He was in bed, seriously ill. The brother had not been at the service either. The great preacher learned that his preaching power was dependent on the prayers of that humble potwasher.

I recall the Sunday my husband and I took my very best friend with us to attend a healing service of the International Order of St. Luke the Physician. My husband had been invited to preach, so I was expecting just to sit in the pew with Betty. As we entered the church, however, a woman said, "Mary, we are so looking forward to hearing you." I had not known I was to speak and told her so. She replied, "Oh, you've got to say something. People are counting on it." That comment could put the "old Adam" to work. Turning to Betty I said, "Start praying while I work up a quick set of notes." She prayed, I worked, and between us we had a presentation ready just in time. I needed Betty and her intercessory prayers. I still do, and I call upon her frequently.

Anyone who wants to function as an intercessor must also allow himself to be prayed for. It's a two-way street. At healing services those who are at the altar praying for others always have others praying for them. Clergy who serve as intercessors for the laity often have the laity intercede for them.

The question often arises "Does the person being prayed for have to know it?" Not necessarily. Jesus sometimes marveled at the faith of those who came on behalf of others. He remarked about their singleness of purpose and their belief that the miracle would happen. Often the one in need of healing did not know of their request.

For almost four years our prayer group prayed for an alcoholic who refused even to admit that he had a problem. He became hostile toward his family, friends, and pastor as they tried to persuade him to seek help. All we could do was pray that the Holy Spirit would somehow lead the man to the point where he would face his problem. We prayed without his knowledge or permission for nearly four years. In the last six months he has done an about-face and sought professional help through Alcoholics Anonymous and the church. A new man in Christ, he has become an evangelist in every sense of the word. "Now " he says, "at the age of fifty, I believe I have a purpose in life. I can help someone else. A flame has been ignited and I know there is power in prayer." Fortunately, our prayer group had not waited for his consent to begin praying for him.

It is advantageous, of course, to have the cooperation and consent of the sick person. Actually, most people welcome, and some request, prayer on their behalf. Intercessors' prayers put windows in the walls we sometimes build around ourselves; they allow the healing Light to flow in.

What if the person prayed for doesn't believe? God does not limit his healing only to the believer. We know that he causes the sun to shine on the just and on the unjust. We know too that Jesus wants healing—wholeness and salvation—for all men. His healing was effective in many cases where the recipient

46

presumably was without faith: the daughter of Jairus, the servant of the Roman officer, the soldier whose ear was healed in the Garden of Gethsemane. Intercessors bring the needy to Christ with no preconditions. They ask for healing in body, mind, and spirit. More than one person has been saved as a result of such prayers and the subsequent physical or mental healing.

This is not to suggest that God inflicts illness in order to bring a person to Christ. What kind of a loving Father would do that? What I am saying is that God can bring good out of any situation. Through Jesus Christ he can redeem an illness and bestow the gift of health and salvation. No man comes to Christ unless the Spirit leads him. We are not to judge how that will come about. We simply pray, trusting the heavenly Father to work in his own way and in his own time.

As individual members of the body of Christ we not only pray, we also witness to the healing power of Christ. When the messengers of John the Baptist came to Jesus he told them, "Go back and tell John what you have seen and heard: the blind can see, the lame can walk, the lepers are made clean, the deaf can hear, the dead are raised to life, and the Good News is preached to the poor. How happy is he who has no doubts about me" (Luke 7:21-23).

I went through a period when I did not want to stand before a group and tell my story. To retell it meant to relive a part of my life I would just as soon forget. So I tried talking about the healing Christ. Inevitably, in the question and answer period which followed my talk, someone would ask, "What happened to you?" The questioner wanted to know my experience with the living Christ. My personal witness was apparently needed to strengthen the questioner's faith. When we share our spiritual blessings with one another we help each other—"You by my faith, and I by your faith" (Rom. 1:12).

People are eager for the witness of the Lord's action in our midst today. Our Lord is a living Lord and he *does* act in our midst today through the Holy Spirit, whom he sent at Pentecost.

Personally, I believe that the gifts of the Spirit, spoken of by Paul in 1 Corinthians, are for every generation of Christians. Like any gift, the gift of healing, if it is to be mine, must be received. And to have meaning it must be used. And to use it is to give witness to it.

Frequently, after a presentation on the healing ministry, individuals will approach me and share an experience they have had with the healing Christ. I always suggest that they tell it to their friends and fellow members: "Tell it right here in this congregation to the other members of the body of Christ." Sometimes people keep their experiences to themselves, fearful that others will think them odd if they give witness to healing. Times are changing in this regard, however, and people are opening up to one another.

A young woman attended our healing services regularly on behalf of her fiance, a cancer victim. For months we joined Lana in praying for Steve's recovery. One Sunday morning Steve received the ultimate healing that comes through death and the resurrection. That evening Lana was at the healing service as usual. She said quite simply, "I want to thank all of you wonderful people who have prayed for both of us through this illness. Now Steve is with his Lord. He is whole and removed from all pain. We should not cry. We should give thanks." Everyone present marveled at her words. She made a wonderful witness to the power of the living Christ working through his congregation.

Christians can serve, not only by intercessions and witness, but also with deeds. It may be as simple a thing as writing a letter. Having written over one thousand letters to individuals seeking help, I've learned first-hand the gratitude people feel—and are willing to express—when someone writes to them in time of need.

A year ago my daughter's sixth grade class "adopted" grandparents who were residents of a local nursing home. The children wrote to their new grandmas and grandpas, and it became a healing adventure. The letters were followed by a visit, relationships were established, and joy and happiness came into lonely lives.

As an intercessor you can also visit shut-ins or people in the institutions and nursing homes. You can even open your own home. Several years ago the phone at our house rang and a voice said, "Are you the lady who entertains foreigners?" The inquirer was a representative of the Episcopal Church trying to find homes for incoming foreign students (especially theological students) for a limited time. Apparently no one on her own parish list was willing to take these students into the home for three to six weeks. She had heard that we hosted an American Field Service student from Norway for one year and had been involved in a YMCA exchange program, so she turned to us.

Over the years our continued participation in her program has opened a whole new world to us. We share in healing the wounds of war and bridging the gaps among peoples of the world. In a single year we have had as many as seventeen house guests (mostly young adults) from many countries, even some who were our "enemies" in time of war. Living with these people, we got to know them as children of God. We came to love them, and now we have "Dear Mom and Dad" letters coming to us from around the world.

Recently we opened our home to an older man who had undergone three major operations (including open-heart surgery) in a three month period of time. He could not be discharged from the hospital unless someone would care for him. Since his family lived far away, we invited him to recuperate with us so he could be near the doctor. His recovery was rapid, and we thank the Lord for using us to help in his healing.

The healing ministry is a way of life for those who are involved in it. We are alert to people's needs. We see brokenness in many forms and do what we can to effect healing. But the body of Christ is more than the individuals in it. It is a community which has a corporate role to play. It functions corporately, not only in the intimate setting of the healing service, but in the ongoing work of the church: maintaining colleges and seminaries, supporting overseas missions, establishing new congregations here at home, providing for the aged (and other social ministries). In so many ways the church contributes richly to the lives of persons and society.

The healing ministry is one part of the total function of the body of Christ. Those of us who are members of this body are called to use our gifts, individually and corporately, for nurturing and being nurtured by the community of faith and witness.

7. The Prayer Group

> ... whenever two of you on earth agree about any-
> thing you pray for, it will be done for you by my
> Father in heaven. For where two or three come
> together in my name, I am there with them.
>
> Matt. 18:19-20

A healing ministry cannot function without the support of a
dedicated prayer group. The formation of such a group is the first
step in any healing ministry. Even where no separate services of
healing are held, prayer groups can be started and can function
effectively to express and implement the healing emphasis in a
parish.

In my experience with establishing prayer groups certain
guidelines have become apparent. In the first place, it is essential
to have the blessing and consent of the pastor. Sometimes a
pastor may have misgivings about the formation and function of a
prayer group. Nevertheless, his advice should be sought and his
judgment considered.

Once the pastor indicates his approval, an initial meeting
should be scheduled for all interested persons. Advance announcement can be made at the Sunday services, in other groups
(the church schools, women's groups, youth groups), in parish
papers, in community newspaper listings of church schedules,
and, of course, by personal invitation among the membership.

The group that responds to such an announcement will
probably be small. Most churchgoers do not want to commit
themselves to a regular and sustained effort. But an interested
group, however small, need not be discouraged. Jesus promised
that where two or three are gathered in his name he will be in
their midst (Matt. 18:19-20).

When the group meets for the first time they should settle on a regular meeting date—after healing services, once a week, twice a month, or they may decide when to meet again at the conclusion of each meeting. It is good to be flexible about the meeting time. The important thing is to meet regularly.

The format for each meeting should be planned in advance lest it become yet another social gathering. For example: the group might study a passage of scripture, review a good book on healing, or study books about prayer. The pastor will be able to give suggestions, but he should not be expected to be the leader.

Part of every prayer group meeting should be devoted to mentioning the names of persons who have requested prayer. The group can also be informed about the status of individuals who are already on the prayer list. Here, confidence is imperative! There should be absolutely no gossip about requests for prayer. Nor should anyone named on the list be asked: "What's wrong with you? I see you're on the prayer list." If an individual wants to reveal the nature of his problem, he should feel free to do so, but he should not be pressured.

There should, of course, be time for actual praying during the meeting. Leading in open prayer may be a new experience for many, so care must be taken not to scare people off by insisting that each person present pray aloud. Silent petitions are prayer as surely as spoken petitions. Rosalind Rinker reports:

> People everywhere have confided to me that they haven't the foggiest notion what to say when they are called upon to pray. Most prayers are such a rapid-get-it-over-with-type thing, that I wonder if they know that prayer is addressing God who is always present *with us*.
>
> "In public prayer, you need only to keep two things in mind, and you will be safe. First, the fact that Jesus Christ is present, because He said He would be there whenever two or three are gathered in His name. So thank Him for His presence; count on it. Second, that His Spirit is present to help and to aid the speaker or teacher, and to help us love one another.*

I know a pastor who has gently and gradually helped his people learn to pray in a group situation. He has each person in the group speak aloud the name of someone to be prayed for. Then the whole group repeats that name in unison, thereby involving the entire membership mentally, spiritually, and verbally in the prayer for that individual. Once I saw him use this approach in an assembly of almost two hundred people. Many individuals participated and some of them told m e afterwards that it was the first time they had ever spoken publicly in a prayer situation.

The next step may be for a prayer group to move on to sentence prayers, each member praying just one sentence aloud. Brevity is the key factor. To pray, "Thank you, Lord, for life" is not too overwhelming even for a new group. Keep in mind that there will always be those to whom spoken prayer comes easily and those for whom it is exceedingly difficult. The Lord welcomes prayer in whatever fashion we offer it—aloud in public, silently in public, or in our own prayer closet.

I was once in a congregation where they had two prayer groups called "Prayer and Share" circles. The first was held in the afternoon and involved praying, sharing, and discussion. The second met in the evening and began with Bible study and discussion. Near the end of the meeting the group formed a huge circle around a chair placed in the center. Anyone who wished could sit in that chair and state his prayer request. Then, whoever felt led to pray for that person got up, went to the chair, laid hands on the person's head and prayed. My first reaction was that this approach would never work. But it did! Person after person walked to the center of the circle and sat in the chair. And person after person went to the one in need and prayed. It was a moving and unforgettable experience.

Prayer groups can experiment with a variety of approaches. It is exciting and refreshing to plunge into a new worship experience knowing the Lord is present to give guidance, hope, and assurance. As acceptance and trust grow within the group, flexibility will grow also.

Once a prayer group has been established, members of the

congregation will call upon it as the need arises. Early one morning my husband received a phone call from a man in our parish: "Pastor, my daughter-in-law had a miscarriage late last night, and early this morning her kidneys stopped functioning. She is in grave danger and the doctor is not too optimistic. Could you pray for her at the service this morning and ask the prayer group to pray for her also?" My husband responded, "Ray, we'll pray for her until she's well." Ray said later that hearing the word "until" had given him great hope. His daughter-in-law not only recovered but has since given birth to two healthy children. In the emergency the parish was available for prayer, and their prayers were effective and appreciated.

At a youth gathering where I was the speaker I was aware of a young man who seemed totally bored throughout my presentation. The thought crossed my mind that he might be there because he had to be. How wrong I was! After the session he approached me in the hallway: "I would like to attend one of your prayer services or a healing service, but I can't because I'm not old enough to drive. On this piece of paper I have written the name of a friend who needs prayer. Would you attend the service and pray for her? I'll be with you in spirit during the time of the service." People do turn to prayer in time of need. A prayer group that is alert and ready can be of help at just such times. Its members become known within the parish and even within the community. People turn to them in time of need.

The healing ministry will be effective only as long as both pastor and prayer group make daily and persistent prayer a priority rather than an afterthought to be used only when it is convenient. Being part of a prayer group is serious business. One must really be willing to make a definite commitment.

Frequently I am asked how long a person should be kept on the prayer list. We keep names on our list for a month with the understanding that the prayer request can then be renewed. Some people have been on our list for several years. Once we discovered that a person for whom we had been praying had inadvertently been left off the prayer list at the end of the month. Each of us thought that the "other fellow" would reintroduce the name. We were not aware of the omission until we heard that the individual's condition was getting worse. In another case a cancer patient on our prayer list was not expected to live; yet she has just returned from a long and taxing trip to the Far East. She believes, as do we, that our daily prayers are part of her treatment; we would not dare remove her name from the prayer list. I cannot explain it, but I know that prayer works. The power of God is limitless. Jesus said that we should always pray and never become discouraged (Luke 18:1).

Again and again I am asked, "How often should I receive laying-on-of-hands and prayers?" I ask in return, "How often should you go to the doctor?" A patient normally sees the doctor regularly until healing occurs. After that he goes for an occasional checkup. The Great Physician longs to see us at least that often.

Some people say, "I don't want to bother the Lord anymore" or "It seems wrong to keep asking." But Jesus tells us that we should not be ashamed to keep asking until we receive what we need (Luke 11:8). A parishioner once complained to my husband, "Why do the Smiths keep coming to the healing services every Sunday, asking the same old prayers for their family week after week?" The Smiths have their own answer: "We are happy that the Lord wants to hear our requests and thanksgivings every week. We believe that our family has stayed well because of our continued asking and thanking. We do not take this love for granted."

Sometimes a person says, "I don't know why anyone should bother about me. What good am I?" You are so good that Jesus died for you! No one should denigrate his own worth in Jesus' sight. The fact that Jesus *died* for our sake makes it quite obvious that every human is worth praying for. Indeed, those who are most unloveable need loving the most.

Jesus told us to love our neighbors as we love ourselves. Our love and care of self is related to our love and care of others. We who bear his name need to set an example, keeping love of self and love of others in balance. A gentleman who apparently felt called upon to make his testimony once said to me, "You got sick because you didn't have the Holy Spirit within you at the time. The devil can't touch me because I have the Spirit's power." Then he spoke at length about the devil, the Holy Spirit, and divine power. As he spoke, it was obvious that the devil carried the man's fork every time he sat down to eat! Like many Americans he was clearly overweight. Obesity generally testifies to poor stewardship regarding the body. "What you are speaks so loudly I can't hear what you say." A Christian's stewardship of his body is a part of his responsibility and witness as a member of a prayer group. His body is the temple of the Holy Spirit and needs to be maintained in a healthy condition if it is to function properly. Discipline in prayer depends upon discipline of the whole person.

The prayer group will be as strong and effective as each member makes it. It matters if a member fails to pray. The day one member misses is the day one link is missing in the prayer chain that surrounds and supports the person in need. From the moment a prayer group is formed, each member must pray that the power of the Holy Spirit will guide and direct the entire group—and then actually allow him to do so.

8. Prayer and Pray-ers

> Pray on every occasion, as the Spirit leads .... keep alert and never give up; pray always for all God's people.
>
> Eph. 6:18

Members of the congregation and members of the prayer group often invite suggestions for establishing their own prayer life. They welcome help in facing some of the perennial questions about prayer.

When do I pray? What is the best time of day? The question is important.

Nighttime is the usual time for most people. Tiredness and sleepiness, however, are not conducive to a concentrated prayer effort. C. S. Lewis observes:

> And, talking of sleepiness, I entirely agree with you that no one in his senses, if he has any power for ordering his own day, would reserve his chief prayer for bedtime—obviously the worst possible hour for any action which needs concentration. The trouble is that thousands of unfortunate people can hardly find any other. Even for us, who are the lucky ones, it is not always easy. My own plan, when hard pressed, is to seize anytime, and place, however unsuitable, in preference to the last waking moment. In a day of traveling—with, perhaps, some ghastly meeting at the end of it—I'd rather pray in a crowded train than put it off till midnight when one reaches a hotel bedroom with aching head and dry throat and one's mind partly in a stupor and partly in a whirl. On other, and slightly less crowded, days a bench in a park, or a back street where one can pace up and down will do."*

Personally, I find the morning a good time to pray. I am thankful for every new day I am given, and I tell the Lord so. I ask that I might be used as a channel for his healing love during the day. And one thing is certain—God is listening! More than once I have asked myself, "How did I ever get into this situation?" The answer has come back, "Mary you offered to be used."

Since prayers can be offered anywhere, anytime, I often use what I call "prayer telegrams." They're short, quick, to-the-point, sentence prayers which I offer throughout the day as I encounter the aged, the ill, the crippled, those who seem to be distressed—anyone in need. One evening, as I sat with my husband in the dining room of the Americana Hotel in New York City, I noticed a young man enter the room and sit down at the next table. He ordered a drink, then sat there and stared at it. Next he ordered a bottle of wine and again just sat there and stared at it. Finally, he drank some wine and then ordered a bottle of champagne. His actions were certainly peculiar. Obviously he had a problem. Should I say something? Should I ignore him? I sent up a "prayer telegram" for direction. Then, sensing that I should say something to him, I was also given the courage to speak. He told me he had reached the point of "just celebrating today." Well, I am all for "celebrating today," but it seemed to me that he was "drowning his sorrows" instead. Our conversation was brief, but I had the definite impression that some healing occurred. A fellow human being had expressed a measure of concern. Someone had cared enough to notice his pain.

A good time to pray is when a person or a need suddenly pops into your mind. Recently the name of a friend who was having marital problems came into my mind several times during a one-week period. Since my friend lives on the west coast, some three thousand miles away, I had no way of knowing if she were in need of a concerted prayer effort at just that time, but I prayed anyway. A week later a letter arrived saying that she and her husband had attended a retreat for married couples and that their problems had been resolved. Coincidence? I think not.

Pray also at appointed times when you are fairly certain you won't be disturbed. If you normally pray in the morning and evening perhaps you could divide your prayer effort, interceding for the sick at one time and dealing with the other concerns during the second period. Sometimes you may find it helpful to go to a service a few minutes early and use that time for intercessory prayer.

These prayer periods do not have to be lengthy. Even several periods a day are not going to disrupt your normal routine. They may give it focus and purpose. The essential thing is to pick a certain time (or times) and adhere to it.

How do I pray? When our prayer group asked that question for the first time we had as many answers as we had people. Each person has his own way of praying. We can, however, learn from others. I find that I am learning and adapting all the time. Some of the things which have helped me may be worth mentioning.

1. Relax. Find a comfortable position. If you can pray better sitting in a chair, by all means do so. If it helps you to put your feet up, do that too. It is far better to sit comfortably and concentrate than to get down on your knees and think only about your hurting knees and aching back. Position can help or it can interfere with your prayers. John Redhead suggests a method of preparation for prayers that begins with what he calls relaxed receptivity.* He takes you, step by step, through the conscious relaxation of each part of the body until, in the final stages, you feel as if you are floating. If you have ever floated in water, you know what total relaxation is.

2. Praise. Once I am relaxed I start my prayers with praise. And there is a difference between praise and thanksgiving. Emily Gardner Neal testifies that she has seen remarkable healing result from this kind of prayer.

> One of the most important spiritual treasures is the healing power in pure praise. I have learned that, important as is the prayer of thanksgiving, even more so is the prayer of adoration. This is the prayer that seems to rise to our lips more and more frequently, and often exclusively, as we become increasingly aware of the holiness and the almightiness and the love of God. This way of prayer, like all prayer, becomes habitual with practice. Praise God whether or not you feel like it and soon you will feel like it. Praise Him simply because He is.*

59

3. Confess. Get the slate wiped clean. As the Psalmist says, "If I had ignored my sin, the Lord would not have listened to me" (Ps. 66:18). We cannot be clear channels of his love if we are clogged up with unconfessed sins. On one occasion I was falsely accused of "talking about someone." The accusation came from a person for whom I had great respect and admiration. It cost me a couple of sleepless nights. I tried in vain to recall what I might have said and how I could have been misunderstood. Knowing how important emotions are in relation to bodily ills, I knew I had to get this straightened out with the Lord. So I confessed my sin of resentment and hurt feelings. I asked the Lord to forgive me for anything I might unknowingly have said or even implied. Finally, I put the individual who had accused me on my prayer list—and the problem itself into my "forgettory," as Dr. Price calls it. Don't hang on to confessed sins. A young man once sought me out: "I've confessed my sins, but I do remember them, and that bothers me. What can I do about it?" I replied, "When you remember them, remember also that they have been forgiven."

4. Forgive. Jesus puts it clearly: "If you do not forgive others, neither will your Father in heaven forgive your sins" (Mark 11:26). Forgiving can be difficult; yet we are told that we must do it. We must not only forgive but also love those who need our forgiveness. Tragically, some people cannot do this. The mother of a drug addict recently said to me, "Our biggest problem is forgiving Kevin for what he has done to us." She fails to see her own involvement in the situation. We are all sinners, enmeshed in the corporate sin of man; this is why we all need to be forgiven—and forgiving. Until all members of the family can grasp their own "sinful saint" position in relation to Kevin's tragedy, I fear he will not be healed. They need not only to forgive him but to be forgiven by him.

5. Intercede. I am sure that we all intercede when we pray; we speak on behalf of others. I cannot believe that any Christian prays only for himself, although praying for oneself is important.

In my own prayers I pray daily for the peoples of the world, for nations, for world leaders, for those who work in advancing the gospel of Christ, and, of course, for my own family, each one by name. I also pray for each person on my prayer list. Most of my prayer is in fact intercessory—on behalf of others.

6. Give thanks. After intercession I give thanks to God for his love. When prayer is offered, God's power is released—a power that is bound to help someone in some way. Thanksgiving should be coupled with intercession even when God's answer to our request may not be what we desired. The sick one for whom we pray may die. Even then we give thanks for God's ultimate healing in death and resurrection. Such prayers of thanksgiving mean much to those in mourning; they bring power at a difficult moment in their lives. Michael Quoist expresses well the basis for such thanksgiving:

> Leaving the cemetery, some of the family were sobbing: "All is finished."
> Others were sniffling: "Come, come, my dear, courage: it's finished!"
> Some friends murmured: "Poor man, that's how we'll all finish."
> And others sighed in relief: "Well, it's finished."
>
> And I was thinking that everything was just beginning.
>
> Yes, he had finished the last rehearsal, but the play was just beginning.
> The years of training were over, but the eternal work was about to start.
> He had just been born to life,
> The real life,
> Life that's going to last,
> Life eternal.
>
> As if there were dead people!
> There are no dead people, Lord.
> There are only the living, on earth and beyond.
> Death exists, Lord,
> But it's nothing but a moment,
> A second, a step,

> The step from provisional to permanent,
> From temporal to eternal.
> As in the death of the child the adolescent is born,
> > from the caterpillar emerges the butterfly,
> > from the grain the full-blown sheath.*

7. Dedicate yourself. Daily I offer myself to the Lord to be used as a channel for his love. As a member of his body, the body of Christ on earth, I offer my particular talents to be used in his service. I read somewhere that dedication can be graded like the stages along the way in school. First comes the kindergarten level: "Now I lay me down to sleep." Second, the grade school level: "Give me, Lord." Third, the high school level: "Show me, Lord." Fourth, the college level: "Make me, Lord." And fifth, the graduate level: "Use me, Lord." It is easy to slip from a higher level of dedication to a lower, but the members of Christ's body in the world are called to function at the highest level of dedication.

8. Pray in Jesus' name. There is power in that name. Our Lord told us that whatever we ask in his name, he would do it (John 14:14-15). Therefore, it comes as no surprise to hear Peter say, as he heals the lame man at the gate of the temple, "It was the power of his name that gave strength to this lame man" (Acts 3:16). As we sing *All hail the power of Jesus' name*, we bring into our prayers that name of matchless power.

The very first time I helped in a healing service the person for whom I was to pray looked up at me and said, "I'm possessed by a demon." The blunt confession came as a shock. I had never really thought much about demon possession from the viewpoint of the healing ministry. There was no time to make inquiries of others, but, thank God, the Holy Spirit came to my aid. Immediately, I recalled how Jesus had cast out demons and how Paul, using Jesus' name, had cast out the evil spirit possessing the slave girl. So I simply prayed, "Release this man in Jesus' name." The following Sunday the man came back and joyfully told us that for the first time in over a year he had been able to return to work. He was free of the demon that possessed him. In our day we do not know what to make of demons. I believe that a demon is a manifestation of the power of evil which can possess a person and separate that person from the love of God. The power of Jesus' name, however, is always greater than the power of the demon.

What do I say when I pray? Again I can only share some suggestions that have been helpful to me.

1. Do not tell God how he should heal. More often than not the visible problem is the product of a different root cause. A man with a terrible pain in his hip and right leg came to a healing mission for counseling. The doctors had told him he would "just have to live with the pain." Yet he had the intuitive feeling that there was something more involved. My husband asked him, "Do you know when this problem first started? Can you relate it to anything else that may have happened at the same time?" Without a moment's hesitation the man replied, "I certainly do. It started three years ago when the state condemned my house for a new highway." As the discussion continued, it became apparent that resentment was his real problem. A prayer for the physical healing of his hip and leg would not have met his real need. He needed healing of the resentment. Since God already knew that, God was asked to heal according to his perfect will. Such a prayer leaves the decision with God.

When we pray, we must be willing to accept the healing God gives. Sometimes the healing of the soul (the "all of me") may require the physical process we call death. This may be the healing process God chooses for enhancing a person's life in that new dimension we call heaven. This too is in accord with his perfect will.

2. Prayers do not have to be lengthy. I remember an incident in my own recovery period which illustrates that a brief prayer is sometimes more helpful. A friend visited me and, before leaving, asked to pray for me. That prayer went on and on and on. Not being very strong yet, I became very weary and silently prayed,

"Lord, make it come to an end so I can get back into bed." Prayers should be short and to the point.

3. Be positive. During my illness I was fortunate to be surrounded by family and friends who were confident I was going to recover. By their positive actions they conveyed that certainty to me. A positive outlook can be contagious. The direction of one's own will can often make the difference between living and dying, so anything that helps the sick person gain confidence is helpful.

My father was a mechanical engineer who lost his job during the Great Depression. He also lost his home and his pride. For a time he dug ditches and huckstered blueberries to support his family. Later he got a job as a milkman. But he was a defeated man. As a result, after an emergency appendectomy, the incision refused to heal. At the time, I was sixteen years old and hoping to become a nurse. Our family doctor, a physician of the old school who treated the person as well as the ailment, took me into my father's room and showed me the open wound. Then he took me out into the corridor and said, "Mary, no doctor can make an incision heal. We have done what we can, but your father has lost his will to live. We can't repair that." My father died.

It all happened so long ago. Yet, it comes back to me vividly even now and raises all kinds of questions. Were we positive when we were around Daddy? Were we positive in our prayers? I think not. Mother was sixteen years younger than my father. She had three daughters to care for at the time. She took in boarders and gave piano and voice lessons to try to keep food in our mouths. As I retrospectively try to put all the pieces together, I realize that we probably surrounded my father with gloom, negativism, and doubt.

When you pray with and for a person, and when you pray alone, be positive. I have found it helpful to picture the person I am praying for as healthy. John Banks suggests:

> Try to see the person as God wants him to be. That is not exactly easy. You may have to take an intermediate step. See him as *you*

would like him to be. Get the mental picture of him at his best. You still do not need to ask God. Deep prayer is communion between you and God. This will be quiet exercise for your imagination. With his help it becomes creative. See Tom cured of his addiction. See Emily recuperating in the hospital. See the nurses, the doctors, the physiotherapists as agents of God's healing restoring her to health. See God working, bringing perfection out of imperfection, order out of disorder, ease out of dis-ease, peace out of turbulence.*

When you think of a loved one who is with the Lord you remember that person in his or her prime. It is also appropriate, when praying for a person who is sick, to visualize that person as being well.

4. Be honest with God. To do otherwise is pointless; it may fool the offender but it cannot fool God. Psalm 139 says in part:

Lord, you have examined, and you know me.
You know everything I do;
    from far away you understand all my thoughts.
You see me, whether I am working or resting;
    you know all my actions.
Even before I speak
    you already know what I will say.
You are around me on every side;
    you protect me with your power.
Your knowledge of me is overwhelming;
    it is too deep for me to understand.

The pray-er must be honest both about himself and about the one for whom he prays. Do not try to diagnose a condition or offer excuses for the person who is sick. Simply commend that person to the Lord, knowing that he knows more about that situation than you do.

5. Bring even the smallest concern to God. People sometimes say, "I'm not going to bother God with that little problem." If people would take all those little problems to the Lord, they might not have to take big ones to him later on. Loving parents who care about their children are eager to hear about their experi-

ences—their joys, their mishaps, and their problems, both little and big. Likewise, our Heavenly Father is interested in every aspect of our lives, and he invites us—indeed urges us—to bring everything to him.

6. Listen. Prayer time should also include a listening time. Scripture admonishes, "Be still and know that I am God." That is good advice, especially in the twentieth century. When we get too busy talking we often forget to listen. In one of his prayers Peter Marshall says, "We know, Father, that we are praying most when we are saying the least."* After you have spoken to God, allow yourself to float in the sea of love with which God surrounds you; be quiet, and hear what the Lord has to say to you in the silence.

In conclusion, I would like to mention that there are many excellent books on prayer (see the book list on page 91). Most give solid advice and counsel to the pray-er. Make up your own book list and share it with others. Since praying is a serious responsibility, each pray-er must try to learn all he can, growing and maturing at his task. It is an ongoing, never-ending process.

9. God's Will in Healing

> ... I am come that they might have life, and that they
> might have it more abundantly.
>
> John 10:10 (KJV)

The question of how sickness, healing, and wholeness relate to
God's will is a difficult one for some people. It could be debated
at length. I speak of it largely out of my own experience.

Some people believe they suffer because God wills it. Others
say that God *permits* suffering, thereby placing the blame at his
doorstep. Christians often conclude their prayer for healing with
the words, "Heal, Lord, if it be your will." Dr. Price calls this the
"escape clause" because it suggests the possibility that perhaps
the Lord does not really want the person healed. And if the
person gets sicker—or dies—the pray-er can then say, "Well, it was
God's will."

Theologians will continue to struggle with the problem of evil
and the problem of pain. My concern is that, psychologically, a
prayer for healing "if it be your will" has a devastating effect on
the sick person. In some cases the patient already suspects that
his illness is God's will; the "escape clause" prayer tends to
confirm his suspicion and weaken his recuperative powers. In
other cases the patient may not have entertained such a notion,
but the prayer raises the question in his mind.

A pastor's wife told me of her experience: "I had a tumor
removed and was recovering quite nicely when someone called on
me and prayed that I would be healed 'if it be God's will.'
Suddenly, I wondered if my caller had been told something I
didn't know. It upset me to the point that it temporarily im-
paired my recovery."

It is sometimes difficult for a person who has never been ill to
understand that *what* we pray is as important as the fact that we

67

pray at all. When I was sick I was acutely aware of what people were saying when they prayed with me. All my "antennae" were out. I read into certain prayers things that were not intended. The last thing a sick person needs is to have doubt put into his mind.

In the ministry of healing we believe that ultimately it is *always* God's will to heal. We say this for two reasons. First, there is no biblical record of anyone ever coming to Jesus for healing and being refused. Second, he tells us to pray, "Thy will be done on earth *as it is in heaven*." Does God tolerate disease, suffering, unhappiness, brokenness, or sorrow in heaven? Of course not. If the petition means anything, it means that God does not will suffering anywhere, anytime.

Since healing involves the whole person we must be extremely careful lest our good intentions—even our well-meant prayers—become the conveyer of illness. Anne White cautions us:

> To say that God allows man freedom of will is not to say that he wills its misuse. God permits sickness, accidents and wars, but he does not intentionally will or cause them. He has to allow man freedom of will or else there would be no true love—it would be coerced. Yet God is always working patiently within circumstances to draw man to voluntary acceptance of His love and of His higher intentional will. He uses our prayers of love and faith as instruments to bring about His ultimate will.*

Emily Gardner Neal writes:

> Try as I might, I could find no evidence to support the belief that a painwrecked body provides a more effective receptacle for spiritual grace. This does not mean that suffering never produces spiritual benefits. Upon occasion it undeniably does. What it does mean, I believe, is that disease and suffering are in no way necessary for spiritual progress. If they were, would Jesus have jeopardized the souls of those who came to Him by alleviating their pain in every instance?*

Whenever I hear a sick person say, "It must be God's will," I wonder why that person even bothers to go to the doctor. If he really believes it is God's will that he should suffer, why does he act contrary to that will and seek medical relief from suffering?

God is a God of love. He is our Heavenly Father. In exercising his fatherhood he exudes love, such love as makes the love of earthly parents pale by comparison. Parents would never willingly send cancer, for example, upon their children. Jesus reminds us that, bad as we are, we do not give our children stones when they ask for bread or snakes when they ask for fish; we know how to give our children good things. How much more will the Father in heaven give good things to those who ask (Matt. 7:9-11).

Sickness, disease, pain—all demand that we reconcile them with our understanding of a compassionate Father. There are times, however, when we simply cannot make the connection. We do not understand or comprehend why a person is not healed. What we do know is that sin, sickness, brokenness, and death came into this world as a result of man's earliest and continuing disobedience. The story of Adam and Eve is your story and mine. As evil is in the world because of human disobedience to God, so suffering is with us as a part of our human condition. It is the condition we must endure as long as we are "in the body," members of a "fallen race."

Jesus treated sickness as an evil intruder, often placing it at Satan's doorstep. He treated illness as something contrary to God's will. In the end, he even dealt with ultimate illness—death. He overcame that final enemy by conquering the grave. In so doing, he provided us with the ultimate victory and the ultimate healing. This is the Father's will.

Jesus' prayer in the Garden of Gethsemane—"not my will but thine be done"—had nothing to do with illness. It was related, rather, to the sacrifice he was being called upon to make. The decision before him had to do with his life's purpose. Was he going to allow the crowd to make him their earthly king? Or was he going to be the "suffering servant?"

When Paul speaks of his "thorn in the flesh" (2 Cor. 12:7)—a figure of speech drawn from the Old Testament where it refers always to the enemies of God—it is not necessary for us to think of a physical problem. It may have been a reference to pride, which Paul readily admits was a problem for him. In any event, the healing Paul needed was apparently received else he would never have endured! God's grace gave him the sufficiency he required so that he could say with the psalmist, "Praise the Lord, my soul! All my being, praise his holy name! He fills my life with good things, so that I stay young and strong like an eagle" (Ps. 103; 1 and 5).

I cannot believe that God ever willed I should have cancer. I do believe, however, that a loving Father redeemed my situation and brought light out of my darkness. He loves me and he loves you. His will is that we "might have life and have it abundantly" (John 10:10)—physical well-being in the second place and total healing in the first.

10. What Happens?

> When John the Baptist heard in prison about Christ's
> works, he sent some of his disciples to him. "Tell us,"
> they asked Jesus, "are you the one John said was
> going to come, or should we expect someone else?"
> Jesus answered: "Go back and tell John what you are
> hearing and seeing: the blind can see, the lame can
> walk, the lepers are made clean, the deaf hear, the
> dead are raised to life, and the Good News is preached
> to the poor. How happy is he who has no doubts
> about me!"
>
> Matt. 11:2-6

What happens when a congregation makes a concentrated effort, through prayer and healing services, to call upon and use the healing power of Christ? That question may best be answered by parish pastors, the people out there on the front line of the church's action. My husband and I are personally acquainted with the situations out of which these pastors speak.

We began healing services in a tentative spirit since we were not sure they would become an ongoing ministry for our congregation. We wanted to see how God would lead us.

Our consideration of the possibility began when our adult-teen discussion group first expressed interest in the concept of so-called faith healing. The group decided to make this a topic of study for a number of weeks. The discussion moved from "faith healing" to "spiritual healing" to "Christ's healing." Members of the group also attended services at a nearby church.

Our first series of special services developed sufficient interest and attendance to justify a continuance. Once we were able to form an ongoing prayer group, we began to hold regular healing services—once a month.

We regard our healing services as a ministry of the body of Christ in this place. Lay people participate with the pastor in the laying-on-of-hands, in praying, in bringing the meditation.

71

HEALING

I believe a healing service is a natural part of the congregation's ministry. It is a means by which the love of God is applied to the needs of the whole person. It is a means of mobilizing the prayers who carry out a ministry of caring for the needs of others.

There have been numerous healings at our services. One woman was healed of a painful inflammation of wrist muscles. There was healing of the relationship between a man and his pastor. Many have been strengthened after the loss of loved ones. People have spoken of receiving a sense of uplift in the midst of deep personal troubles. Others have felt added strength as they underwent surgery.

We know that the healing service is not a substitute for medical or psychological help, but it is one more vehicle through which God can work in situations of need. A woman who attended a healing service for the first time reflected, "There was a real feeling of peace in the service." *Shalom*, the Hebrew word for peace, includes both physical and spiritual well being. This is what people experience in a healing service.

G. Milton Johnson, Pastor
Gethsemane Lutheran Church
Plainfield, New Jersey

After twenty-three years of pastoral service I found that I had begun to have a feeling of disillusionment, a feeling shared by many other experienced ministers. My ministry was beginning to grow stale and mechanical. I even wondered secretly what I believed.

About that time I had the privilege of hearing Dr. Price speak on our Lord's challenge to preach, teach, and heal. He said that while many of us in the ministry are faithful in preaching and teaching, we are literally ignorant and "unbelieving" when it comes to healing.

Not long after that I began to read books on spiritual healing, most notably *A Reporter Finds God Through Spiritual Healing* by Emily Gardner Neal. I can say candidly that my interest in healing was stimulated, but I was afraid to get involved. Nevertheless, I found myself conversing with some of my parishioners about it, trying inconspicuously to test their reaction.

One day the telephone rang in my study, and an elder of the church asked me point blank, "Do you really believe in spiritual healing?" Immediately, I suspected some ulterior motive. I hoped he would not get to the point, but he did: "I have a heart condition which I have never told you about before, but I would like to receive anointing and laying-on-of-hands." I was scared. Perspiration began to appear on the palms of my hands. I asked him when he wanted this done. "Tonight," he answered. "You mean this very night?" I asked. "Yes," he said, "*this* night." I hardly ate a thing for supper. I was ashamed to admit my nervousness even to myself.

That evening was a milestone in my life. Though nervous and perspiring, I anointed a fellow Christian for the first time in my ministry. It was a brief and private service. When he got up off his knees he looked me squarely in the eye and said, "You'll never know what this has meant to me. I know that I'm going to be better physically and spiritually." Then he added, "When are we going to begin public services of spiritual healing?"

Two months later we began special services of healing at our church. At first I was afraid no one would come; later I was afraid too many would come. And those who came were not those I would have expected. They were simply people who turned to the church in their need.

In the ensuing four years I have seen attendance grow from twenty-three to an average of two hundred—from all denominations. The corporate character of the body of Christ has really become meaningful to me. Healing services are beyond denominationalism. Ecumenism has never been more real to me than it is now.

Charles M. Fitz, Pastor
Second Presbyterian Church
Elizabeth, New Jersey

HEALING

We hold a service of healing the last Sunday of every month. Both clergy and laity participate in the prayers and in placing oil upon the foreheads of worshippers. We have not attempted to publicize our healing ministry in special ways, for we consider it an ordinary part of our ongoing parish life. Nevertheless, many of us feel the mysterious power of the Holy Spirit surging into our lives, healing diseases, and helping people with problems and decisions. The congregation now seems to be working together where in the past we were pulling apart. Our one goal is clear: to witness to the love, joy, and peace we receive only through our Lord.

In April a man who had undergone surgery for cancer three years ago found evidence of another tumor. The fiftieth wedding anniversary was a sad occasion for him and his wife; they were told he would have to return to the Johns Hopkins Clinic to undergo the same tests as before. Immediately our "Prayer and Share" group was notified, and his name was presented to the Lord. By August his tumor was gone. The doctor told him it was the first time in forty years as a doctor that he had seen a tumor of that size completely disappear. The day our group learned the happy news we were all in one accord in praising God for "our miracle."

A child born to grateful parents in our congregation was not expected to live because of internal complications. The parents brought their child with them to the healing service. It was the first they had attended, and many people prayed for them that night. Months later the child is now well and happy—to the bafflement of the pediatrician who says she can't understand it. We can! And we praise God for his healing power.

We believe in doctors, of course; they are God's instruments of specialized healing. But we believe also in the Master Physician, our Lord and Savior. Our congregation seeks to preach, teach, *and* heal—all through the Holy Spirit, and in the name of Jesus Christ, begotten of the Father.

William J. McCabe, Pastor
Emmanuel Lutheran Church
New Philadelphia, Ohio

In our complex and rapidly changing society people carry a wide range of problems and burdens. They have an intense hunger for reality, often expressed in a search for more intimate and less cognitive ways of "knowing." People are interested in an active theology in which they can participate. Whereas an older generation was encouraged to *think*, people today are urged to *touch*.

It is against the backdrop of this contemporary setting that I note the benefits of the healing ministry.

For me it has meant a fresh vitality in my preaching. Illustrations flow from my deeper sharing with parishioners and friends. I can proclaim God's healing power with confidence since I have seen it at work.

House calls are more interesting and more productive. Members ask questions that probe the areas of honest doubt, unhealed memories, resentments, jealousy, guilt, and boredom. Often this discussion leads to prayer, and laying-on-of-hands right there in the home.

A satisfying result of my involvement in the healing ministry has been stimulating dialogue with people in the medical and social professions as we search for a working partnership. I no longer evade the physician's question, "Just what can you as a clergyman offer a sick person?"

I have come to appreciate the Holy Communion as a main channel for releasing God's healing power into individual lives and relationships. This happens repeatedly, especially when the service includes the laying-on-of-hands.

The ministry of healing is clearly preventive as well as curative. People in robust good health attend our services to keep themselves well! The greatest benefits are enjoyed by persons who perceive that this ministry is for the healthy as well as the infirm. To them it is not an optional or peripheral matter but essential to their parish life and worship.

Samuel E. Purdy, Rector
St. Peter's Episcopal Church
Mountain Lakes, New Jersey

Our monthly community service of healing exists because of the commitment of three pastors, eight lay persons (including a medical doctor), and the power of the Holy Spirit working through us. Representatives from Methodist, Lutheran, United Church of Christ, and Church of the Brethren congregations work together in planning and leading the services. We met many times before we held the first service. We needed to compare and develop our understanding of healing and identify several areas of differences. A diverse group, we found that we were able to survive only through the power of God's Spirit and our common commitment to spiritual healing.

Individuals have been healed. A core of persons is committed to attending regularly. People come expecting God's healing presence. We sense the togetherness of the corporate body of Christ.

Most of our "regulars" are members of traditional churches and were initially suspicious of a healing service. They felt that such services were alarmingly unorthodox. Even in traditional churches, however, there is developing an awareness that God heals through a carefully developed service of healing. Also, the term "divine healing" is more and more often being extended to include community health concerns and even the reconciliation of power conflicts in political and governmental structures.

As we gain experience in spiritual healing, we find new questions emerging. The result is that we sponsor an annual healing mission, at which we spend a whole weekend exploring these questions in depth. We try to undergird the spiritual dynamics of healing with solid theology in order that we do not drift into unhealthy ruts or become blind to our own sicknesses. Many people in our town thank God for the healing power he offers us through the services of healing.

Fred L. Shilling, Co-founder
and first Executive Director of the
Association for Creative Change
Hummelstown, Pennsylvania

76

Healing services offer our too competitive and alienated society—and churches—an alternative way of sharing our problems. At such services each worshipper feels a little less alone with his trouble. The atmosphere of trust is therapeutic in itself. Needed healing forces are at work in the sermon and the testimonies. Stating one's problem privately at the altar rail personalizes God's concern. Traditional church people are not intimate or trustful enough to be comfortable with deep sharing. Therefore "mutual consolation of the brethren" is often neglected.

We pastors should not feel threatened by the healing services our people attend. We each have our own gifts in the areas of personal intimacy, counseling, visitation, and preaching. None of us can be all things to all people. We should welcome interchurch specialization in administering the gifts of the Spirit.

The healthy healer and the truly healed strike a balance between personalized ministry and social concern. Those who minister best to individuals in personalized ways also support social action. And the best leaders of social justice movements have a genuine empathy with individuals facing personal problems.

From my point of view, there is a time to pray for the miraculous, for tissue to be created ex nihilo. That time is when all other avenues of healing have been exhausted. So far my prayers for such miracles have been to no avail, but I will continue to pray for them from time to time.

There is also a time, however, to *not* pray for the miraculous. We must remember that "it is appointed unto man once to die." Lazarus died and so did everyone else whom Jesus ever raised or healed. I would not normally pray for limbs and organs to grow on maimed, deformed, retarded, or aged bodies. Such prayers, for me, would be inappropriate, a temptation to anticipate what is really reserved for the resurrected life. Our prayers must be for healing *and* for discernment, so that we may properly commit to God's hands the mysteries of death and irreversible handicaps.

77

HEALING

There is also a time to thank God for the help he provides through medical science. The doctor is God's man-on-the-spot in many cases. You do not pray a shattered body together after an auto accident; you do not pray a transplant or a transfusion. You pray for the doctor. And a praying doctor is a special blessing!

Gerhardt Kugler, Pastor
St. John's Lutheran Church
Union City, New Jersey

More than 175 persons were present for the first healing service. As the invitation was given for persons to come to the altar rail for personal prayers, people not only filled the front of the chancel but, in every case, personally expressed the problem they had brought with them. I was amazed!

Worship at Trinity had for too long been a spectator sport. I would defend the validity of public confession, general prayer, and all the corporate aspects of worship, but not to the exclusion of private expression of personal needs. The response to the healing service demonstrated to me that our people will come forward and express their individual needs in the context of public worship.

We at Trinity have not continued the healing services. By default the healing ministry is again being neglected in our midst. Why? As pastor I have wrestled with this. Is it fear of failure? Is it an unwillingness to trust God and believe he can heal? I think I'm afraid "to let go and let God" in this matter of healing ministry— and that bothers me. But I am still open, and I am determined not to allow the abuses among some "healers" to dissuade me from taking seriously such an integral part of our Lord's ministry.

Elton P. Richards, Pastor
Trinity Lutheran Church
Reading, Pennsylvania

Our people have absorbed the concept of the healing of the whole person. They do not look for physical healing only. Their requests run the gamut of individual needs. And real healing is taking place.

One woman, who faithfully attends each monthly service, informs me that according to her doctor her cancer has not increased and, in fact, may be diminishing. A man who prayed for his critically ill mother believes that her recovery is the result of what happened at the healing service he attended. A woman reports that her depressed and ailing mother has taken a complete turn for the better, both physically and emotionally, after she was prayed for at the healing service. Another woman's cancerous condition has not improved, but she and her husband have said: "Pastor, whether or not the physical condition improves we already have been healed." A doctor and his distraught wife attended the healing service two days before she underwent a radical mastectomy. On the night before the surgery, and again the day after, I found her completely calm and trusting. She had an inner strength I would not have anticipated. She has been healed "on the inside," and we continue to pray that physical healing will follow.

Each service of healing is a moving experience. Men, women, and young people have been helped. While this aspect of the church's ministry should never take the place of the ministry of Word and Sacrament, there is, I feel, a real place for it.

The Rev. Dr. Robert S. Romeis, Pastor
St. John's Lutheran Church
Sacramento, California

A Service of Healing

Leader: Hear what our Lord Jesus Christ says, "Heal the sick and say to the people, 'The Kingdom of God has come near you.' When you pray and ask for something, believe that you have received it, and everything will be given you."

Hear also what the apostle James says, "Is there any one of you who is sick? He should call the church elders, who will pray for him and pour oil on him in the name of the Lord. This prayer, made in faith, will save the sick man: The Lord will restore him to health, and the sins he has committed will be forgiven."

Hear what the apostle Paul says, "Do not conform outwardly to the standards of this world, but let God transform you inwardly by a complete change of your mind."

Then shall a Psalm be read responsively. Appropriate Psalms are: 20, 23, 91, 103.

Then shall be read a lesson from scripture.

INTERCESSIONS

Leader: Seeing that we have a great High Priest, Jesus Christ, the Son of God, let us come boldly to the throne of grace, that we may obtain mercy and find grace to help in time of need.
The Lord be with you.

People: And with you, too.

Leader: Let us pray.

All: Our Father . . .

Leader: Remembering that all of God's children are near and dear to him, wherever they may be, let us first pray for those who desire our prayers, many of whom cannot be with us this day.

A SERVICE OF HEALING

Here shall be named those who desire prayer to be made for them.

Let us pray for those who are ill in body, distressed in mind, or troubled in spirit.

Blessed Jesus, we bring into your loving care and protection, on the stretchers of our prayers, all those who are sick in mind, body, or spirit. Take from them all fears and help them to put their trust in you, that they may feel beneath them and around them your strong and everlasting arms.

Cleanse them of all resentments, jealousy, self-pity, pride, or anything else that might block your healing power. Fill them with a sense of your loving presence, that they may experience the kingdom of love in their whole being. Touch them with your divine, transforming power, that they may be healed and live to glorify you, to be used by you to build your kingdom on earth.

People: Amen.

Leader: Let us now pray for ourselves, first putting ourselves— body, mind, and spirit—in the healing presence of Christ.

Then shall silence be kept for a time.

Leader: Lord, hear our prayer.

People: And let our requests come unto you.

AFFIRMATION

Leader: O Lord, save your people.

People: They put their trust in you.

Leader: Send them your help.

People: And always give them strength.

Leader: As I live in Christ I am supplied with all the spiritual resources required for my needs.

People: As I live in Christ I am free from fear and have quietness and confidence within.

Leader: As I live in Christ I am at one with God and know the peace of God which passes human understanding.

People: I can do all things through Christ who gives me strength.

Leader: I believe in the Son of God; therefore, I am in him.

People: Give peace for all time, O Lord, and fill men everywhere with the Spirit of our Lord Jesus Christ.

Leader: Who shall separate us from the love of Christ? Shall tribulations or distress, or persecution, or famine, or nakedness, or peril, or sword?

All: No, in all of these things we are more than conquerors through him who loves us. For I am persuaded that neither death, nor life, nor angels, nor principalities, nor powers, nor things present, nor things to come, nor height, nor depth, nor any other creature shall be able to separate us from the love of God which is in Christ Jesus our Lord.

CONFESSION OF SINS

Leader: Let us humbly confess our sins to God.

In our confession let us think, not only of the sins of commission, but also of the sins of omission. Let us think, not only of the gross sins, but of the sins of disposition as well: bitterness, worry, hurt feelings, resentment, jealousy, spiritual pride, living in the past, self-love, self-pity.

Let us also acknowledge our involvement in the corporate sins of our day, the problems that plague mankind: war, poverty, ignorance, discrimination, and delinquency.

All: O Almighty God, Lord of all, we confess that we have sinned against you in thought, word, and deed. Have mercy upon us, O God. According to your great love do away with our offenses and forgive us all our sins, for the sake of Jesus Christ. Amen.

THE ABSOLUTION

Leader: The almighty, loving, and merciful God now gives you absolution and remission of all your sins.

People: Amen.

Then shall follow a sermon.

ANOINTING AND LAYING-ON-OF-HANDS

Leader: The Almighty Lord, who gives power and strength to all who put their trust in him, be now and evermore your defender; the Almighty Lord, to whom all things in heaven, in earth, and under the earth do bow in obedience, instill an assurance within you that there is no other name but the name of our Lord Jesus Christ whereby you may receive health and salvation.

People: Amen.

Then shall the people come forward for the anointing, laying-on-of-hands, and prayers at the altar rail, after which they shall return to their places.

THANKSGIVING

Leader: Lift up your hearts.

People: We lift them up to the Lord.

Leader: Let us give thanks to our Lord God.

People: It is the right thing to do.

Leader: It is very right, and it is our grateful duty, to give thanks to you, O Lord, our Father, who gives us health and salvation; whose son came into the world that we might have life, and have it in abundance; who in his love for all men ministered to

their bodily infirmities, and gave both power and command-
ment to his disciples to heal the sick. We give you hearty
thanks and praise that you have this day continued your
healing work among us. Make us ever mindful of your mercies,
that we may continue to be your faithful servants to the end
of our lives, through Jesus Christ, our Lord.

People: Amen.

BENEDICTION

Leader: God the Father, God the Son, God the Holy Spirit,
bless, preserve, and keep you; the Lord look with his merciful
face upon you, and fill you with his grace, that you may so
live in this life that you may have everlasting life.

People: Amen.

A Brief Service of Healing

Scripture and Meditation

THE PROMISES OF GOD

Leader: Listen to the promises of our Lord Jesus Christ:
"Truly I say to you, if you have faith as a grain of mustard
seed, you shall say to this mountain, be removed; and it shall
remove; and no thing shall be impossible for you."

People: Lord, I believe; help my unbelief.

Leader: Our Lord called the twelve together, gave them power
and authority over all demons, and gave them power to cure
diseases. He sent them forth to preach the Kingdom of God
and to heal the sick. After these things the Lord appointed
seventy others, and he said to them, "Into whatever city you
go . . . heal the sick that are there, and say to them, 'the
Kingdom of God is come to you.' "

People: Lord, I believe; help my unbelief.

Leader: Listen to the words of St. James, the apostle of
Christ: "Is any among you sick? Let him call for the elders of
the church; and let them pray over him, anointing him with oil
in the name of the Lord; and the prayer of faith shall save him
who is sick, and the Lord shall raise him up and if he has
committed sins, it shall be forgiven him. Confess, therefore,
your sins one to another, and pray one for another, that you
may be healed."

People: Lord, I believe; help my unbelief.

THE CONFESSION AND ABSOLUTION

Leader: Almighty God, Father of our Lord Jesus Christ, Creator of all things, Judge of all men: we admit the sins of thought, word, and deed which we in our self-centeredness, have committed.

People: Forgive us for Christ's sake. Forgive us all that is past, and help us to serve and please you in newness of life.

Leader: Almighty God, our loving Father, who in his love has promised us forgiveness, does now forgive you.

People: Amen.

PRAYER FOR HEALING

Here shall be named those who desire prayer to be made for them.

Leader: Let us pray.

O Almighty Father, who heals the bodies and the minds and the spirits of human beings, who sent the Lord Jesus Christ to heal every disease and sickness and to redeem us from death: deliver your servants from all infirmities of body, mind, and spirit; quicken them by your love and presence, for you are the fountain of healing, O Lord God.

People: Amen.

All: Our Father . . .

Leader: At this time worshippers may kneel at the altar rail for the anointing, the laying-on-of-hands, and personal prayers.

A CORPORATE RESPONSE

All: Psalm 23 (in unison)

THE BENEDICTION

Leader: Our Lord Jesus Christ preserve you in body and mind and spirit, until the last day.

People: Amen.

Notes

Page

5. Emily Gardner Neal, *A Reporter Finds God Through Spiritual Healing* (New York: Morehouse-Barlow, 1956).

9. Martin J. Heinecken, *Basic Christian Teachings* (Philadelphia: Fortress Press, 1949), p. 34.

11. Genevieve Parkhurst, *Healing the Whole Person* (New York: Morehouse-Barlow, 1968).

12. Howard and Martha Lewis, *Psychosomatics* (New York: Viking, 1972).

13. Rollo May, *Power and Innocence* (New York: W. W. Norton and Co., 1972), p. 14.

14. Emily Gardner Neal, *Where There's Smoke* (copyright © 1967 by Morehouse-Barlow Co., Inc., 14 East 41st Street, New York, N.Y. 10017), pp. 129-130. Used by permission.

17. Anne S. White, *Healing Adventure* (Evesham, England: Arthur James, 1969), p. 23. Used by permission.

18. *Ibid.*, p. 22.

24. Paul Tillich, *The Eternal Now* (New York: Charles Scribners Sons, 1956), pp. 58-65. Used by permission.

24. Neal, *Where There's Smoke*, p. 45.

28. Dennis J. Bennett, *Nine O'clock in the Morning* (copyright © 1970 by Logos International, Plainfield, N.J. 07060), p. 101. Reprinted by permission.

29. Weekly Church Bulletin Service (Philadelphia: Fortress Press, October 18, 1970).

31. Morton T. Kelsey, *Healing and Christianity* (New York: Harper & Row, 1973), p. 80. Used by permission.

31. "Sacrament for the Sick" *Time* (5 February 1973), p. 65.

Reprinted by permission from TIME, The Weekly News Magazine, copyright Time Inc.

34. John Sutherland Bonnell, *Do You Want to be Healed?* (New York: Harper & Row, 1968), p. 89. Used by permission.

37. Neal, *Where There's Smoke*, pp. 100-101.

38. *The Holy Communion*, Contemporary Worship, no. 2 (Philadelphia: Board of Publication, Lutheran Church in America, 1970), p. 35.

38. Bonnell, *Do You Want to be Healed?*

42. Peter S. Ford, *The Healing Trinity* (New York: Harper & Row, 1971), p. 58. Used by permission.

43. Malcolm H. Miner, *Healing is for Real* (copyright © 1972 by Morehouse-Barlow Co., Inc., 14 East 41st Street, New York, N.Y. 10017), p. 21. Used by permission.

52. Rosalind Rinker, *Praying Together* (copyright © 1968 by Zondervan Publishing House), p. 60. Used by permission.

57. C. S. Lewis, *Letters to Malcolm: Chiefly on Prayer* (New York: Harcourt, Brace and World, 1963), pp. 16-17. Copyright © 1968 by Harcourt Brace Jovanovich, Inc. Used by permission.

59. John A. Redhead, *Letting God Help You* (Nashville: Abingdon Press, 1957).

59. Neal, *Where There's Smoke*, p. 57.

62. Michael Quoist, *Prayers* (New York: Sheed and Ward, 1963), pp. 41-42. Copyright © 1963, Sheed and Ward, Inc., New York. Used by permission.

65. John Gaynor Banks, *Healing Everywhere* (Logansport, Indiana: Saint Luke's Press, 1961), p. 186.

66. Peter Marshall, *The Prayers of Peter Marshall*, ed. Catherine Marshall (New York: McGraw-Hill Book Co., 1949), p. 15. Copyright © 1949 by McGraw-Hill Book Co. Used by permission.

68. White, *Healing Adventure*, pp. 29-30.

68. Neal, *A Reporter Finds God*, p. 94.

Additional Books on Healing

Blackburn, Laurence H. *God Wants You to be Well.* New York: Morehouse-Barlow, 1970.

Doniger, Simon. *Healing: Human and Divine.* New York: Association Press, 1957.

Frost, Evelyn. *Christian Healing.* London: A. R. Mowbray and Co., 1954.

Kuhlman, Kathryn. *I Believe in Miracles.* Old Tappan, N.J.: Fleming H. Revell Co., Spire Books, 1969.

Large, John Ellis. *The Church and Healing.* Cincinnati: Forward Movement Publications, 1965.

Marshall, Catherine. *Beyond Ourselves.* New York: McGraw-Hill Book Co., 1961.

Martin, Bernard. *The Healing Ministry in the Church.* Richmond: John Knox Press, 1960.

Neal, Emily Gardner. *God Can Heal You Now.* Englewood Cliffs, N.J.: Prentice-Hall, 1958.

Parker, William R. *Prayer Can Change Your Life.* Englewood Cliffs, N.J.: Prentice-Hall, 1957.

Sanford, Agnes. *The Healing Light.* St. Paul: Macalaster Park Publishing Co., 1947.

———. *Sealed Orders.* Plainfield, N.J.: Logos International, 1972.

Spraggett, Allen. *The Woman Who Believes in Miracles.* Cleveland: The World Publishing Co., 1970.

Swaim, Loring T. *Arthritis, Medicine and the Spiritual Laws.* Toronto: Ambassador Books Ltd., 1962.

Tournier, Paul. *A Doctor's Casebook in the Light of the Bible.* New York: Harper & Row, 1960.

———. *The Meaning of Persons.* New York: Harper & Row, 1957.

HEALING

Weatherhead, Leslie D. *Psychology, Religion, and Healing.* Nashville: Abingdon Press, 1962.

Westberg, Granger E. *Minister and Doctor Meet,* New York: Harper & Row, 1961.

Scripture Index

HEALING

Colossians
4:2—54

Hebrews
10:36—56

James
5:14-16—35
5:14-16—43
5:16—62